crazy
lucky
girl

Maeve —
Looking forward to helping you with your project. Hope you enjoy!

Jen

SUSAN MEITNER

crazy lucky girl

Do *YOU* Have
the Keys to
Success?

Advantage®

Published by Advantage, Charleston, South Carolina.
Member of Advantage Media Group.

ADVANTAGE is a registered trademark and the Advantage colophon is a trademark of Advantage Media Group, Inc.

Printed in the United States of America.

ISBN: 978-1-59932-444-9
LCCN: 2014946841

This publication is designed to provide accurate and authoritative information in regard to the subject matter covered. It is sold with the understanding that the publisher is not engaged in rendering legal, accounting, or other professional services. If legal advice or other expert assistance is required, the services of a competent professional person should be sought.

Illustrations by Brenda McCallum.

Advantage Media Group is proud to be a part of the Tree Neutral® program. Tree Neutral offsets the number of trees consumed in the production and printing of this book by taking proactive steps such as planting trees in direct proportion to the number of trees used to print books. To learn more about Tree Neutral, please visit **www.treeneutral.com**. To learn more about Advantage's commitment to being a responsible steward of the environment, please visit **www.advantagefamily.com/green**

Advantage Media Group is a publisher of business, self-improvement, and professional development books and online learning. We help entrepreneurs, business leaders, and professionals share their Stories, Passion, and Knowledge to help others Learn & Grow. Do you have a manuscript or book idea that you would like us to consider for publishing? Please visit **advantagefamily.com** or call **1.866.775.1696.**

Dedicated with Love . . . xoxoxo

To my family, especially my wonderful parents: I have become the person I am today due to your amazing support, trust, guidance, and unconditional love. I hope I can pave the way for Drew and Allyson as you did for me! I am blessed to have parents like both of you.

To my amazing children, Drew and Allyson: I am beyond proud of the individuals you are growing up to be. I am sure you will achieve anything you set your minds to. You both make me smile and I am truly thankful every day.

To my brother, Tory: For all of the ups and downs, you are the best brother anyone could ask for in this world. I especially love that you think I am so funny!

To David: You know just how "crazy" I am and you love me anyway. That makes me a truly "lucky girl."

ACKNOWLEDGMENTS

· ·

I would like to acknowledge a few people for assisting me in the creation of this book: John, my mentor in this crazy business, for constantly serving as a sounding board for me and for your endless editorial skills and creative wisdom; Steven, for your encouragement and wisdom when it comes to direction and guidance, which I so relied on with this book and many other issues; and Melissa, for helping pull everything together when time was of the essence and keeping everything on track.

I thank all of my Centennial Lending Group family!

CONTENTS

· ·

CHAPTER 1

. . . .

It's Like Dating

Crazy lucky girl: Believe me. I have been called worse. I tell people all the time that selling is like dating. You have to be a little crazy, and you have to be a little bit lucky. Some may find the key to success through their girlish charms or their manly dispositions, but they also have to be good. They have to be good people and good at what they do. At Centennial Lending Group, affectionately known as CLG, we are all about mortgages. Mortgage lending is not something you major in at college. I am pretty sure most children do not race home one day and tell their parents their dream is to become a loan officer. It is one of those sales careers people enter because they are self-motivated to make a good income and because they are naturally competitive. Oh, and they are a little crazy and a little bit lucky.

If someone had told me five years ago that I would be the CEO of a company, I would not have believed them. "It is just not possible," I would have said. Then again, I also never imagined the mortgage industry would suit my personality as well as it does, or that running a business could be as rewarding and as exciting as it is. It really is fun and, in the pages of this book, I will tell you why.

I went to a private Catholic school through my entire childhood, and I always felt I was trying to keep up. I finally came into my own as an adult. In high school I was not the smartest girl, or the prettiest, and I was not the most popular. As we approached graduation, I became increasingly anxious about my class ranking. My school was an all-girl, private high school with 88 graduating seniors. When class rankings were announced, I was in the bottom quarter of the class, and that was not fun. I think, however, it had everything to do with why I am so competitive now.

I have two children: Drew, who is 13, and Allyson, who is 11. My children are athletic and competitive, which is interesting, because I was not that way as a child. It is a running joke that I would coerce my parents into writing notes in elementary school and high school to get me out of gym class. I am competitive now, but I did not discover my true competitiveness until my professional life was underway. When I went "out on the street" as a salesperson in the mortgage business, it started my competitive juices flowing.

I have come to realize that I need continuity in my surroundings, in my family life, and in my social life. I find it tremendously comforting. For instance, I live in the same county where I grew up, just outside Philadelphia. I went to college in Virginia, but I eventually moved back to the suburbs of Philadelphia. I still remember how I agonized over whether to return to the Philadelphia area or remain in Virginia.

My four years in college were a wonderful experience. While at college, I was the social chair of my sorority. It is an ideal job for someone like me, your classic people pleaser, which is what I have always been. If I gave any thought to my career during college, it was to picture myself as a professional event planner. Truth be told, I pictured myself as the organizer of White House dinners. I ended up doing well academically and socially, and I thoroughly enjoyed my college experience.

From time to time, I am invited to come back to my former high school, Gwynedd Mercy High School, to speak to students on career day about being a mortgage loan officer. When in front of the group, I will sometimes make the statement that mortgages are sexy. I do it, in part, for the shock effect. If you do not hit them with a comment like that, you will have trouble keeping students interested in such a topic, much less in prompting them to consider a career in mortgage lending. Most young girls I speak to want to be doctors, lawyers, broadcasters, or advertising executives, all of those supposedly cool careers.

They always take my bait, though. When I call mortgages "sexy," a hand will go up and at least one student will be intrigued enough to ask, "How can mortgages be sexy?" Then, I turn it around and ask my own questions.

I say, "How many people here have been told by Mom and Dad that they cannot ask people how old they are?" The girl with her hand up says, "I would never ask people how old they are." It is not polite, right? Then, "Is it okay to ask for a person's Social Security number?" I will get another no. Is it okay to ask people where they live and how long they have lived there, or how many children they have, where they work, and how much money they make? Oh, no. You cannot ask that. It is too personal. Can you get them to tell you how much money they have in the bank? Will they tell you whether they own their car or lease it, if they own a vacation home, or if their credit cards have high balances? How about getting a copy of their divorce agreement?

Will they hand over their bank statements, pay stubs, work history, and a whole stack of other personal information? How about getting people to share personal secrets that may make them feel ashamed of predicaments they got themselves into? Will they admit they have made some terribly bad business decisions or have bad credit as a result of a risky decision, or an unlucky break?

By this point, I have their attention. I tell them, "In my business, we pull back the curtains and lift up the skirts and that can be fun, sexy almost! If you ask people for enough personal information, before long, they are standing pretty much naked in front of you. I am able to ask all those questions each and every day and make the people in front of me feel relatively comfortable while doing it. They develop a trust with me. I think it is because I appreciate how uncomfortable it can be to share such information. That is how a great salesperson sells—all salespeople, not just loan officers. A good salesperson makes people do some things they may not feel comfortable doing, such as providing sensitive personal information when they are buying a car, or a house, or whatever. The salesperson needs to be able to elicit that information in a low-stress, conversational way. By the way, it is a fantastic job if you are an inquisitive, borderline-nosy person, as long as you always handle it professionally and confidentially."

Then I tell the girls I get to ask questions people are not usually allowed to ask. I get to figure out how to help the people I am working with purchase their dream house, and they love me for it. I tell the girls, "I actually am getting paid for being nosy!" They laugh. I, in essence, am laying the groundwork to become their mortgage consultant for life.

When I talk to salespeople, I make the case that mortgages are sexy because I always equate what happens in mortgage sales, or any sales for that matter, to dating. Revealing ourselves is uncomfortable for all of us. It happens when we are dating and it happens when we get a mortgage. One of the loan officers at Centennial Lending Group, the company I started, recently came to me with a problem. He could not get any realtors to give him referrals or leads for mortgages. I asked him, "How are you going about it?" He said, "Well, you have been telling me that I need to *ask* for the business, so I go in and ask for the business. I start up a conversation with a realtor, saying, 'We do a great job. I really can use the business, and I need you to try me, so will you do this for me?'"

To help him out, I brought up the scenario of a nightclub where he might see, across the bar, a girl he would like to date. "Do you walk over and say, 'I really need to date you, and you need to date me?'" I asked him. He said he would never do that. "And supposing you were with a girl and having a great time on the first date, would you say flat out, 'I would like to sleep with you tonight?'" And he said, "No, of course I would never say that. I would get slapped."

I nodded my head and gave him a moment to reflect. Then I told him he was getting slapped down by the realtors because no realtor is going to give a loan officer business if they sense he is desperate. For someone to *want* to give business to you, you have to exude confidence, give the impression *everyone* in town is asking for you, continually referring business to you, and wanting to work with you and you only. It is similar to per-suading a girl she should go out with you. If people around town aren't talking and making a fuss about you, you've got work to do.

I hit him with that basic reality. Men who are dating, I told him, need to take a woman out for drinks. They need to wine and dine her, buy her coffee, call her, get to first base, second base—all those things, right? He saw where I was going with this and nodded in agreement. "The effort you make while dating is just like the effort you make in selling," I continued. "You show up at a realtor's office with a great attitude. You invite that realtor to lunch and eventually to a happy hour. Then, by the third meeting, you should have laid enough groundwork to say, 'You know what? I'd love the opportunity to do business with you. Why don't we do a deal together? That would be so much fun.' And before you know it, they *want* to do business with you. Then, you can watch as the referrals come your way."

This is the way I have always done it. I am not sure how I hit on this strategy, but it always seemed to work for me. It is because developing trust is a slow process. This is true for any sales position. Also, in a male-dominated business, this strategy has always worked because, I think, a woman has a distinct advantage. Men inherently believe that saleswomen can be trusted with their information. They are inclined to believe women care. That being said, people have to like and trust a salesperson, male or female, in order to work with that person.

I like to think somewhere along the line in the courtship approach to selling I also indicate I will conduct myself with integrity. You have to earn people's ongoing trust, or you are nowhere. Integrity is the key. Obviously, the mortgage industry, in general, made huge mistakes in the past. When I was thinking about trust and what I should write, I wanted to make it clear I have never put borrowers in a loan that was not right for them. I was in the thick of things while the mortgage business was imploding, but that was not my doing. There was a time when it was almost shameful to admit to

> *"People have to like and trust you in order to do business with you. You must build a relationship with integrity to get consistent future business."*

being in the mortgage industry. I would have to preface it by saying, "I never wrote any of those bad mortgages."

Part of the reason for the downfall of the economy back in 2008 was a push for low- or no-documentation mortgages. Those loans did not make sense, and anyone with half a brain knew they were a recipe for disaster. I could not bring myself to make such a loan, even though the government, through Fannie Mae and Freddie Mac, was encouraging us to do so. They told everyone to utilize their automated underwriting system. No longer were we required to provide backup—or any documentation, for that matter—on some files. If the system did not ask for more information, we had no worries. We simply just moved on. Most of the news coverage of the mortgage meltdown leaves out that part of the story.

From a regulatory or government standpoint, things got very loose, fast, and easy—one pay stub, one W-2, one bank statement, good to go. As long as the borrowers signed a document attesting to their stated income, nothing else was necessary. Well, it was fine as long as people were telling the truth. It was anything but fine once people decided to abuse the system and the automated underwriting did not ask for much more than a pay stub or a W-2, if that. The computer does not necessarily know the person behind the loan or her respective industry. The computer does not think to ask more questions. The computer never came back and said, "I am sorry, but the city bus driver probably does not make $100,000 a year."

A good salesperson knows their industry, and mine requires me to evaluate credit risk, debts, and liabilities. Debt is a funny thing. Some people hate it and some people do not mind it. I happen to love debt, although it has to be properly structured and covered so the borrower can afford the bills. I have six mortgages myself, so I eat what I cook. Debt that is handled properly can create wealth. However, it requires discipline and consistency. Running a company that is predicated on credit risk can be very challenging. You have to be a creative problem solver, but you also need consistency in your daily practices. I truly feel, as long as all concerned know where they stand, they are better off—in any situation. I try to instill that in my staff. I encourage them to make sure all parties in the transaction know where they stand and how their status may change. Sometimes, this means asking a lot of questions. It is all about keeping everyone informed and managing expectations.

Someone once told me I ask a lot of questions and I keep asking until I get the answer I want. To a degree, that is true, but I need to understand fully what is being asked and how my opinion can affect a situation. I do not make any decision until I have all the background information, and only then am I able weigh the various options. Some people think a smart person knows all the answers. However, a very smart person once told me that when you ask questions, you actually sound smarter. If you are just acting as if you know, when in fact you do not know, that will eventually catch up with you and bite you. In the same vein, it is okay to say, "I do

"Manage expectations— underpromise and overdeliver in every part of the transaction."

not know the answer to that, but I will be sure to get back to you with the right answer." That being said, you have to find the correct information and promptly call the inquirer back. When this is accomplished, you immediately develop a trust and demonstrate you bring value to your customer. When you show you care enough to go the extra mile, it speaks volumes.

. . . .

We all live by certain ideals and beliefs, and, if you are lucky, those come to light early on through family. Very few have been mentored and supported by their family the way I have in my life. My mom is a stay-at-home mother who believes her job is her children and her grandchildren. She makes dinner every night. This is the way I was raised, and I love the fact that my children too have this experience, as her grandchildren. My father is an attorney and he will say that he is just a good ol' country lawyer, but that is not the half of it. He owns his own law firm and was always his own boss. My dad has a phenomenal sense of community and a solid-gold reputation in the area where he works, the same community where we live. My parents supported my brother and me to no end. My family lives on what people teasingly call "the compound"—everyone but me, that is. My brother and his wife, their children, and my parents all live on the same property. When my grandmother was alive, she lived there as well. I talk to my mom at least once every other day and I see my parents throughout the week. We are a very close, tight-knit family.

My adult life is not quite the same as the one I had growing up. I am a divorced mother of two children. My son, Drew, and my daughter, Allyson, are the lights of my life. Although I am fond of saying that nothing is perfect, my children are as close to perfect as they can be, for me. Allyson was born hearing impaired and this discovery marked a truly difficult time in our lives. I was definitely challenged to keep my family and work life together. We have come to understand Allyson is a child first and a child with a hearing loss second. A little before the age of two, she received a cochlear implant, which allows her to hear. This was a big decision for my family. Having your infant undergo surgery that involved drilling into her skull for hours was difficult, but her resultant hearing was well worth it. Yet hearing was not an immediate result of the surgery. Allyson had hours, days, and months of therapy to teach her how to hear and listen. There were years of bringing Allyson back and forth from school, which was over an hour away. These are just some of the little things we do for our children. I am one of Allyson's biggest advocates. I want both of my children to learn from watching me. As long as they continue to strive to achieve, I am confident they will succeed.

When I look at my motivation in business, I see it has many facets. A driving force is my children. I make a point of letting them know anything they set their mind to can be achieved in time with hard work. It is a matter of doing something even when you do not know how to do it. Somehow, you have to figure it out. That is a guiding principle for me, and I want it to be for my children as well. As Drew and Allyson grow older, I watch each of them taking notice of how our family interacts and, at the same time, of how my office is growing. They watch intently and ask relevant questions for children their age. I strive to make sure I set a great example for them. As young as they are, they keep me in check. I love their curiosity and the sparkle in their eyes when something clicks. As I watch my children grow up, I try to do things right, both at home and at work. My "moral compass," my gauge of what is right and what is wrong, is a set of values etched in me by my parents at a very young age.

I feel reassured most of the time that my moral compass points true north, and ethically, we are on very sound footings at Centennial Lending Group. The company was launched because there was no other place, in my opinion, for me to work where I felt comfortable. I believe ethical standards must be maintained at all times, and I could not find an environment where I felt certain that was the case. When I first decided to become an entrepreneur, I made a list of all of the things I liked and all the things I did not like at each of my former companies. I have tried to implement the aspects I liked, and I've made a point of eliminating the things I did not like. This simple list has guided us on many decisions we have made at Centennial Lending Group.

I have always felt loyalty and openness are important traits. I tend to wear my emotions on my sleeve. I treat our staff and our salespeople the same way I treat my customers. I like to learn their stories. I don't deal with every single customer at Centennial Lending Group anymore, but over the past two decades, I have written thousands of mortgages. To this day, when I go to the local mall or go to the grocery store, I run into people whose mortgages I did and I love catching up with them. It is all about trust and the relationships that you build.

You build on those relationships if people feel you have been genuine with them.

By nature, I'm a deeply loyal person. When the time would come for me to move on in my career, it was always difficult for me. Along the way, I've had people act in a manner that I viewed as disloyal, and I must admit it is an unpleasant, empty feeling for me. That said, early in my career, I made the decision to leave my job and walk away from the person who was my mentor in the industry. Although this episode eventually had a happy ending, it also taught me to put myself in someone else's shoes, to better understand why he was upset. Sometimes you need to balance your own moral compass in order to understand someone else's. You need to be empathetic toward others, especially those who have had a major impact on your life.

Empathy is one characteristic that is sometimes missing in a boss or a salesperson. We are all human and we all have weaknesses. At times, we can become quite vulnerable. Over the course of 20-plus years, I feel as if I have seen and heard just about everything, but to this day, I still can be caught off guard. I have attended mortgage settlements in which the husband failed to disclose he was making support payments for a child from a previous marriage. Buying a house is an important, and tricky, moment in life. You need to understand what is going on in the lives of those you are trying to help. The pressure is on, and you need to be sincere and bring a caring attitude to the borrowers. Being empathetic is part of being a thoughtful, considerate person and having humility. You have to be outgoing and want the best for people, especially those who are nervous and not familiar with the process. When customers realize I can relate to what they are going through, they trust me even more. I know I constantly revisit this need for trust, but if people are not open and honest, others will not trust them with their friendship, and they will most certainly not trust them with their business. I believe trust is what makes customers continue to come back to me.

A few months ago, I was contacted by a customer whose mortgage I had done 12 years earlier. He sent an e-mail, saying, "Hey, Sue, haven't talked to you in a while, but I'm thinking about refinancing my house and rolling my equity line into my regular mortgage, and possibly pulling some money out." It was very satisfying to receive that e-mail. This happens frequently, and it makes my day every single time. You try so hard to build trust and confidence, and when it works, it is a wonderful thing. In our business, we ask customers to provide us with sensitive information. If they fail to do so, we can hit a wall at an extremely inconvenient point later in the process. I have found that if they trust us, they will not hold back

> *"Show empathy and compassion during the process to make your customers feel you understand their situation."*

necessary information about their finances, their work, or their personal history. People will give you all of their information as long as they feel they can trust you, knowing their information is secure and confidential. In return, I make sure their experience ends up being a positive one. The gentleman who contacted me after 12 years must have had a world-class experience with me, or I would never have heard back from him. This is a huge part of developing consistency in any business.

The other lesson here is to keep in touch with your past customers. As with any type of sales, when a past customer uses your services several times and refers you to friends and family, that is the best compliment of all. So you need to be good, ethical, empathetic, and honest. If you can demonstrate those qualities and still bring a high level of energy to the job, you will be very successful. I learned this early in my career as a mortgage salesperson. I was, and still am, highly competitive. Earlier in my career, after developing a taste for being the top loan officer in the office, first on a monthly basis and subsequently on an annual basis, I did not ever want to give that up and, fortunately, I never did.

The first time I ever earned the distinction of being top sales person was at a company called Philadelphia Financial. Another loan officer, who had been number one for years, commented under her breath, "one-year wonder," implying this honor would not be awarded me again. She didn't realize I had heard her comment. Neither did she realize just how much her remark fueled my desire to continue to be number one. Maintaining the number-one slot lasted well over a decade for me. I refused to give it up. Through all the variables of bringing up children, caring for a child with a special need, having a bad marriage—through everything—the constant was my business and maintaining my number-one status. It was a driving goal I tried to achieve every year while I did what I loved to do: write mortgage applications to help people get the house of their dreams. To this day, I love every aspect of the mortgage business. I feel I was able to maintain these goals because I wrote them down and mapped how I would achieve each goal during the good times and the bad. My plan, and the fact that someone thought I could not accomplish my goal, motivated me to achieve even further-reaching goals. The key is to figure out what your goals are and to work toward each one.

I love having a realtor tell me, "Oh, the other mortgage company couldn't get it done." I love to be the mortgage person who gets the difficult loan to the settlement table when another lender could not. A hard-working salesperson and a reasonable customer make a great combination. I have always felt that you are only as good as your reputation. Believe it or not, once you have really made your name, you can actually make a mistake and people will tend to forgive you. Honest mistakes are okay, which is another lesson I try to pass along to my children and to our employees, even though, right now, in the mortgage industry, there is little if any room for error when handling a mortgage.

We want our salespeople to compete in the market-place with complete confidence, knowing they have the best support team behind them. They can say with such assurance that Centennial Lending Group has the most knowledgeable and dedicated staff in the business. Recruiting great people in sales and operations, we believe, enhances our ability to handle even more business. Our salespeople can say we do everything in-house. We have the best underwriters, the best processors, and the best closers in the business. To have the best people working right under one roof, each and every day, is what makes this all so different, all so worthwhile. All of this allows us to go the extra mile for our customers every time.

We all work hard, and I can honestly say that quality of life for our employees is a priority. Quality of life includes work and home. It is a constant balancing act, one I have struggled with. I have had very good luck and many good breaks, yet there has been a cost to everything I have built and learned over the years. For instance, one of my business decisions cost me a very dear friend. I felt that loss to my core. Sometimes the lines get blurred between the business and personal worlds. Friendships are dear to me. It is painful to lose a friend because of professional choices. Sometimes, however, you need to just move forward, despite the pain and the hurt. You have no choice but to keep moving forward. In doing so, you can build great momentum. At Centennial Lending Group, we keep this in mind. The sweetest of all sweet spots happens when hard work and opportunity meet.

SUE'S CORE BELIEFS:

· ·

CHAPTER 2

Face Your Fears and You Will Find Your Strengths

I went to the same private Catholic elementary school to which I now send my children. I believe it is an important rite of passage. My mother tends to point out that in my years as a student there, I complained often about how strict it was, and not much has changed. She asked me, "What makes you think your children will enjoy it any more than you did when you were their age?" My answer is that I want them to grow up well balanced more than I want them to enjoy themselves. The school does a great job of instilling the values learned at home. I believe this is vital in raising young children today. My children's school continues to teach the same values I learned all those years ago, and that I still live by to this day. It is a safe haven for them, and I wouldn't have it any other way.

When I graduated from high school, I decided to attend George Mason University in Fairfax, Virginia. George Mason is an enormous university, with 30,000 students from virtually every corner of the globe. I remember, one August day, we loaded up the family car and drove to Fairfax for my freshman orientation. We were only on campus for a very short while when my mom turned to my dad and said, "It's time to go." My father was baffled. "What do you mean we are leaving? We just got here! I thought we were going through orientation with Sue and helping her to sign up for her classes." My mother told him no, they needed to leave. She said they had "things to do."

They said their goodbyes, got back in the car, and headed for home. Years later, my mother explained her reasoning to me. At the time, she was convinced I would have come right back home with them if they had not left at that moment. I would have made a decision not to go away to college at all. She could tell by the blank expression on my face I was overwhelmed. The thought of being so far away from home, surrounded by these strangers from all over the world, could very well have pushed me over the edge. Somehow, she knew I was so close to saying I could not stay and would they please take me straight home.

Suddenly, I realized I was the only member of my family still on the George Mason University campus. It was a harsh reality for me. For the very first time in my life, I was alone. "I don't know anyone!" I thought. "How could I have signed up for this? How could I have put myself into this awful situation?" I wandered aimlessly around campus and eventually walked into a classroom with a lecture underway. I sat down next to a girl. The stupor I had fallen into was interrupted when she said, "Wow, you have a lot of freckles."

I turned and looked at the girl, who was smiling at me. "So do I," she said enthusiastically. I said, "You're right, we definitely have lots of freckles." That is exactly how I wound up meeting my absolute best friend for life. Her name is Hasty. She is actually more like a sister than a friend. Since that first day of freshman orientation, we have had a special bond. It turned out meeting Hasty in that classroom was a huge life event for me. So was the decision we both made, a few minutes later, to say yes to an interesting opportunity.

We were asked to go on a leadership retreat the first weekend of school. So, instead of being with the entire freshman class, getting tours of the dorms and the dining hall, off we went to a leadership retreat that resulted in being introduced to every president of every organization on the George Mason University campus—yes, every sorority, every fraternity, every club, the campus newspaper, the yearbook, everything. It was good to be lucky.

After that weekend, Hasty and I went directly into sorority rush. We had a distinct advantage over other pledges in that we had already met the various sorority presidents and made friends with them. It was great for my self-assurance to know I had developed a friendship with the president of the school newspaper, among others. In spite of being new, I already knew many people on campus. I found it interesting to talk to everyone about anything and everything. It was a rewarding experience and it had a strong impact on our future activities and opportunities at George Mason University. We still have life-long connections because of that initial weekend. The bonds and connections that were developed proved extremely fruitful throughout college and after.

Back then, no students planned their careers until the senior year, unless they knew exactly what they wanted to do for the rest of their lives. I was never sure what I should do with my life, but I was fortunate to be working for a good company while at college. During my time at George Mason, I worked at The Gap. While there, I was selected for an internship and they groomed me for their management program. I worked at The Gap when I was not in class and after graduation.

Working for The Gap was like being part of a corporate cult. I would attend training workshops and seminars at which they taught us how to sell and how to manage people. I learned all about the various products and gained extensive knowledge from the training. In hindsight, the training has helped me ever since. I have worked most of my life, from the time I was 15 years old. My parents did not require me to work, but I loved working and I still do. At The Gap, I learned to hire 200 people for the Christmas holidays and then lay 120 of them off after Christmas. I was taught to let them go in a way that convinced them it was in their best interests.

When I graduated from George Mason in 1992, I took the job that was waiting for me as a Gap store manager. It was the path of least resistance, and it seemed to be the right move for me. It was going really well until I was fired. I ended up being dismissed after just five months. Getting fired, at such an early age, was a traumatic experience. I remember how horrible I felt. However, in retrospect, it ended up becoming a positive event in my life, though I certainly did not feel that way at the time.

Looking back, I can tell you that I was never going to be a great retail store manager. They had policies and rules that I did not agree with, and I did not understand the logic behind them. The loss of paychecks made me panic. So, the next day, I applied for unemployment benefits. The line of people stretched so far I could not see the end of it. I also could not see myself getting into it. So, I did not. I said to myself, "I am sure it is easier to get another job than to go through this." I had not experienced many failures in my life, and getting fired by The Gap qualified as a relatively big one at the time. I had a conversation with my father and he convinced me, after some protesting on my part, that I should come back home to figure out what to do next.

The next move was prompted by Dad's introducing me to a man who managed a mortgage company. His name was John Crits, and he allowed me to shadow him for one day. He explained to me what a mortgage salesperson did on a day-in, day-out basis. He asked me if I was interested in learning his business from the inside out, and I said yes. I went in for a second interview with his partner and they offered me an entry-level position in the office, with a starting salary of $23,000. However, there was a catch.

The other partner wanted to hire another woman he had recently interviewed. They hired both of us but came up with a competition to see who should actually end up with the position, which was that of a post-closer. Post-closers, typically, take over after all the documents have been signed at settlement. The signed papers come back to the mortgage company, and they have to be stacked in a specific order before being sent to headquarters, where someone checks the work. Our task was to take the collection of papers, stack it in a specific order, make a copy of each one, and ship the stack to an investor, who would then purchase the loan from the company. We had to do as many as we could within one day.

I should tell you now that, at the time, I did not know how to spell the word *mortgage*. I had no idea what went into a mortgage. Nonetheless, I learned quickly and I ended up getting the job. That was probably the first time I was really competitive in business; to keep the job, I had no choice but to compete. It was also another fear faced and conquered, and little did I know the strength it showed at the time. Understanding that came later.

John had a major impact on my career, and he taught me a great deal about the business and the attitudes associated with the business. He taught me about the pitfalls of the business. Back then, he called me Gap Girl and, in general, he was pretty tough on me. But I did learn. Among the life lessons he taught me is one I still utilize to this day. As a result of that experience, I believe the best place to start in the mortgage business is in the post-closing department. You must become familiar with all the mortgage papers and understand what they mean.

In addition, if there is a problem, you must figure out how to resolve the problem before the file is shipped out of the office.

Today, I'm the CEO of a mortgage company, and yet, as a result of that past experience, I can do virtually any job in our office. Whether it be post-closing or underwriting, I can jump right in to lend a hand. My staff knows I will work alongside them when necessary. I believe this allows me to develop strong relationships with them. The message I send is this: no matter what the situation, I will always help if it means getting an issue resolved. I am never too proud to do the work myself—not bad for a girl who did not know how to spell the word *mortgage*.

When I went to work for John, the economy was weak. Layoffs were common. One day, John brought me into his office and said, "You have a choice. You can either continue working here as a member of the support team and face the possibility that we may eventually need to lay you off, or you can consider becoming a salesperson for us." There was a brief pause, and he said, "I know it is earlier than you would have liked, but I think you're ready for it." He figured I would be up for the challenge. He wanted me seriously to consider it. He said, "They're building a lot of new houses in Bucks County. We need to send someone into that territory and go after that business. We think you're the right person for the job."

"Never let your ego get in the way of business."

Hmmm . . . scary.

When I asked about compensation, he told me I would be going from making $28,000, my salary at the time, to making as much or as little as my loan closings would generate. I told him that sounded like a situation where, if I closed zero loans, I would make zero salary. He said that was about the size of it.

Hmmm . . . even scarier.

I went home to think about this and discuss it with my family. My dad took the position that staying on staff, which seemed the safest bet, really was not safe at all, and had a very limited upside. "I think you need to be a salesperson," he said to me. "You need to be in control of the amount of money you can earn." I told him that it might add up to nothing, but he, as always, was supportive of me and confident of my abilities. He persuaded me to take advantage of this new opportunity. I took his advice. When we finished talking, I knew I was about to embark on a new chapter in my life. From that moment on, I have never looked back. I could feel my competitive fires starting to burn. The move may have been scary, but I was finally in control of my destiny. I was nervous but really excited about the future opportunities.

CHAPTER 3

· ·

Rejection

O ver time, I have learned that rejection today is just that: rejection today. Tomorrow will be another day, and if you forge ahead, the next day may well bring lots of business your way, as long as you never settle. You must constantly keep pushing yourself to reach your goals.

I started working in the mortgage industry in October 1992. Just two years later, I found myself out on the street selling mortgages. By 1997 I was selling enough to earn more than triple the amount I initially made as a staff person. Even in my first year, I earned more than I would have earned in my job as a processor. In the beginning, though, I must admit, it was pretty daunting. I did not have a salary, because I worked 100 percent on commissions. I had no settlements, and thus no commissions, so I did not have any money at all. I remember having to ask John to advance me $100 to pay my credit card bill. I did not like asking him and I never asked again.

When I first went "on the street," John knew I could get by on my enthusiasm alone for a while. It was how I countered my obvious lack of experience. His strategy for me was pretty simple. New construction was gaining momentum in various counties, including Bucks County, an area just north of us where we needed representation. So, that is exactly what I did: I represented. I walked into real estate office after real estate office and talked to whoever would listen. In those days, if you were fortunate enough to receive leads, you would actually meet the prospective buyers at their home or apartment. Quickly, I learned this was an important step.

I soon discovered these meetings to get the mortgage process started significantly enhanced a prospective borrower's chances of having his offer accepted when he bid on a house. The house sellers always felt more comfortable when a prospective buyer was preapproved by a mortgage company. Additionally, I discovered these prompt customer meetings almost always allowed me to secure the mortgage. This was because I could start developing a relationship with the prospective buyers. I began a dialog with the buyers and was allowed to recommend their bid be accepted on a specific house. These were very valuable lessons. I remember a time when I pulled up to the house of a customer who said, "Young Lady, you don't seem old enough to be giving me a mortgage."

I replied, "Sir, I'm glad to meet you. My name is Sue Meitner, and I actually *am* old enough to give you a mortgage." Bernard has since refinanced his Doylestown house, bought another house, and refinanced two more times, with me. I was not willing to let him reject me because of my age. Bernard, to this day, is one of my lifetime customers. I think he liked my spunk.

Certain personality types are drawn to this kind of work. To be good requires knowledge and expertise about lending, credit, property transfers, and so forth. You have to be on top of things, smart, and detail oriented. You also need to be a quick learner. Almost everything is on-the-job training. Once you have gained experience, you keep building on that wealth of knowledge, gaining more and more confidence as you go. Knowing your customers and what makes them tick is essential.

"Try to develop a relationship with your customers to turn them into raving fans!"

The real estate business teaches you about people and real-life situations. You can become quite skeptical or even cynical when working as a loan officer. There is a lot of rejection in this business. It is no coincidence that *Glengarry Glen Ross*, David Mamet's classic play (and screenplay), showing hyper-competitive salespeople, is about selling residential real estate. When it comes to making deals come together, the pressure is real. The mortgage is, typically, the glue that makes it all work. Dealing with pressures from both the borrowers and the realtors is standard operating procedure in our industry. How you handle such pressure is what sets you apart from the competition. You are, in essence, responsible for handling and orchestrating the largest and most important purchase that most people will ever make. It is not something to be taken lightly.

In the mid-1990s you would leave rate sheets when you paid a visit to a real estate office. Since rates changed daily, we constantly updated and printed new ones. I always considered them personal billboards, in that my name and phone number were prominently displayed on them. I would walk into a real estate office and introduce myself to the staff and ask them to keep me in mind for any of their mortgage needs. I would then ask to place a rate sheet in each of their mailboxes, making polite conversation as I did so. How times have changed. We did not communicate daily via e-mail, even though this is a great way to follow up with realtors and borrowers.

Going out to realtor's officers with a rate sheet would not be my current advice to a new loan officer, but in those days, it opened the door for me to start to make a name for myself in an unknown market. I still encourage loan officers to visit real estate offices frequently and to shake as many hands as possible. Even if those offices have an in-house arrangement with another mortgage company, you can still pursue the business. You have to be prepared to go in and save the day if that company does not perform and drops the ball. This does happen. You just have to be ready and available at a moment's notice.

The mortgage world is small. People constantly change companies and take advantage of new opportunities. Everyone in the business seems to know everyone else. Mortgages are expensive commodities. That said, competition exists—*lots* of it. One day, during my first few months as an originator, I went into a national real estate office to say hello and drop off rate sheets. The person at the front desk said he would need 11 of them. I pulled the rate sheets out of my briefcase and said, "Where should I put them?" He said, "Just hand them to me and I'll show you exactly where they go." I handed him the sheets and he crumpled them up and threw them in the trash. "That's where we put your rate sheets," he told me.

I was shocked, but I put up a brave face. "Thanks for letting me know that," I told him. "I really appreciate it. If you should ever need my help, just let me know." Then I walked to my car and tried to pull myself together. I called John and let him know what had just happened. He told me I needed, eventually, to go back through that door again and "own that office." I had to demonstrate I was serious about covering the territory and I had to commit to visiting that office now more than ever. "In the meantime," he said, "keep your chin up and drive yourself to the next office and walk right in. The next one will go better." He was right.

Over time, I got my footing. I found my groove. I ended up developing *my style*. I perfected my elevator speech. You know the speech, the one you give when you only have one to three minutes to get it all out. Well, I perfected it! And it never sounded rehearsed; I always tailored it a little to the person I was speaking to. After a while, things naturally got more comfortable. I quickly learned the importance of developing a relationship with the person at the front desk in addition to the agents.

You will experience a lot of rejection at first, but eventually, everyone will welcome you into their world if you are persistent. They know when you are young and working hard, cold turkey calling is not easy.

I gained confidence the hard way and knew I would end up being a good salesperson, because I really enjoyed it. I enjoyed meeting new people. I enjoyed building and solidifying relationships. Rejection actually motivated me to work even harder.

The agents saw how hard I worked and how tenacious I was, and I received referrals. I felt that I had finally arrived. I knew I was helping people and providing stellar service. I felt needed. Most importantly, I was having fun. I loved the different situations I had to handle every day.

In any business situation—business-to-business, in particular—if the company you are soliciting has a certain need that is being filled adequately by a supplier or a vendor, you will be told, "Well, gee, we already have a vendor or supplier who does that for us." At this point you can say, "That's great and I definitely don't want to infringe on that in any way. In fact, I respect loyalty as much as anyone, but if there ever is a need or a situation where I can help, please keep me in mind." As it

"Competition is healthy and should be a positive."

turns out, that need happens just about every day. Nothing is sweeter than a telephone call from a real estate office that already has an in-house mortgage company or a lender they like to recommend, and they cannot get the loan to the settlement table on time. Centennial Lending Group continues to "save the day" in those instances, every time. I take pride in knowing we can easily close a loan in two weeks when necessary. We deliver great service. All I need to do is make sure everyone else knows.

I knew that I was going to be a successful salesperson when, early in my career, I lost a million dollars in business in one day and took it in stride. In mortgage sales, you can always lose deals after you take the application because of a better rate or lower fees somewhere else, or because the customer decided to do business with a friend of a friend. There are many ways to lose a loan. On this particular day, all the planets lined up wrong. When I counted the deals that had gone south, it came to $1.2 million! This was during a period when I would get upset if I lost a deal worth $200,000 or $300,000. The thought of losing $1.2 million would usually cause me to have a complete emotional meltdown.

After a few seconds, I sat back, took a breath, and looked around. Instead of being upset, I thought about how the various deals had fallen through and analyzed them a bit. I just was not getting all that emotional over it. I think there was a voice in my head saying, "You're going to be okay." Of course, I would. There was plenty of business out there and I had no problem going after it.

Here is how it happens: You get into a flow; you find a rhythm, and good things start to happen. If you are not in a flow, you have to do something differently, fast. Having a positive attitude goes a long way toward achieving your rhythm. To this day, I tell salespeople how to go about getting into a groove. The market may be slow, but not you. Every January I worked hard so that, come February, I would be taking at least one application a day. This was my goal. When February was over, I would have at least 28 new applications. This turned out to be a very effective strategy, a pace setter for my entire year. I did this each and every February. Rejection never entered the equation. Failure was not an option for me.

One way or another I just had to reach the 28-applications goal, and that is what I did.

"Write down all your goals. You have a much better chance of achieving your goals when they are written down and you can refer to them often."

I have often been asked, "How do you get into a rhythm when there is no activity in the market?" The answer is you need to meet lots of realtors and any other referral sources you can think of visiting. Put yourself out there. In December, attend as many holiday parties as you possibly can. Call your past customers, visit real estate attorneys, and talk to accountants and financial planners. Divorce attorneys can be an excellent source of business. People divorce throughout the year. When they get divorced, they typically need to refinance because one of the spouses is eager to buy out the other one. Also, take full advantage of social media marketing. This is a vital tool in the market today. Centennial Lending Group has had, for years, a department dedicated to marketing and social media.

I never knew I was going to sell mortgages, but if selling were going to be my profession, why would I not want to sell something most Americans need? You could sell insurance, but people hate paying insurance premiums, whereas they recognize the importance of obtaining a mortgage.

People appreciate great service, but sometimes they need to be reminded good service is not always the norm. When people regularly see you in their real estate office, they realize you are in it for the long haul. They realize you are vested in succeeding in the mortgage business. They notice the amount of business you are doing. Eventually, someone will realize, "Sue is at our office all the time. She must be very good." At this point the realtor might decide to give me a chance. It is persistence, but it is also the wow factor! Make sure to look great when you meet with potential referral sources. Walking into a real estate office can be difficult and awkward. It is not always fun. Be confident. Convince the realtors that you are a person worth talking to, worth knowing. It works.

"Attend all your settlements. They are the best place to ask for referrals and shine."

I was out recently, having a drink with our sales manager. A competitor of ours was sitting next to us. Instinctively, my sales manager went in for the kill and said, "You should come talk to us," meaning that competitor should consider leaving his current position to work at Centennial Lending Group. My instinct was to nip this in the bud. I chimed in, "No, no, if you're happy where you are, you should definitely stay there."

As we left, my sales manager, John, asked me why I took that approach. "That guy is eventually going to work for us," I said, "if we want him to. I just don't want him to think we are desperate, if you get what I mean." I left the door open, but I wanted to let that guy make a move on his own timetable. Nine times out of ten this strategy works, partly because everybody thinks the grass is greener on the other side.

I tell my staff that if they think the grass is greener elsewhere, who knows, maybe it is greener. If they do not think Centennial Lending Group is the best company for them, I would prefer they go and be happy elsewhere. I want my staff to *want* to work at Centennial Lending Group. If someone resigns, he usually gives me two weeks' notice. Sometimes I choose to take the two weeks and other times I choose to have the employee leave immediately, because I simply do not tolerate drama. We try to have a strict no-drama policy in my

"Avoid drama at all costs."

office, because drama makes me crazy (and not the good type of crazy). It cuts into all productivity, which no one can afford. I suspect this is the same for most businesses. If I sense drama, I address it immediately with an all-hands-on-deck management meeting.

Drama takes up too much time and energy, which is completely unproductive. We need to make sure everything gets to the settlement table on time. Talking to and meeting with the borrowers is important, and the originator has to set expectations and get all their information. Some people in our business make it look easy. That, however, can become a double-edged sword. Some make it look so easy that it seems as though anybody can do it, which could not be further from the truth. Make no mistake, this job requires you to wear multiple hats; it requires a lot of hard work. I have come to discover the ones who have the perfect system, and are proficient in what they do.

I find I rarely make little mistakes. When I make a mistake, it is usually a huge one, but that is part of on-the-job training. This, I find, is true for a new salesperson, right up to a CEO. Fortunately, I seldom make the same mistake twice. I always tell new loan officers, "If you think you're not going to make mistakes, you are delusional. You're going to make mistakes. You just need to address and tackle those mistakes head on." Making mistakes is part of the territory and how we know we are human. The key, when a mistake is made, is to address the mistake as fast as it can be addressed and have a solution for fixing it. I always try to have a plan A and a plan B for all situations.

Loan officers can utilize different, but equally effective, methods and styles. A technically minded person is probably not going to be the best one to go out there and become successful in mortgage sales. Usually, an outgoing, highly sociable person excels in sales, someone who does not mind working on a 100 percent commission basis, who can handle rejection, who exudes confidence, and who says, "I'm going to get you to the settlement table." There might be some bumps in the road because, usually, we have to comply with many different regulations. An experienced mortgage professional can navigate through minefields. I always tell people if they hear from me during the process, it means we are not getting everything we need to approve the loan. Loan applicants, other than at the time of their mortgage application and during the settlement, really do not want to hear from me. That is the perfect mortgage process. Most mortgage applications, however, are not perfect—far from it, in fact. You will, for sure, hear from the processor regarding such things as missing items or questions that need to be answered.

In my early years as a loan officer, I made mistakes and I learned from them. I also learned how to develop my style of communication. I developed techniques for building my business. I was able to experiment, always knowing that John was in charge and running the company competently. I felt as though John was looking out for me and protecting me. This gave me tremendous professional security, but at some point, it just wasn't enough. I needed more in my career. I soon realized I wanted to go out on my own as a manager and see what else might be out in the big mortgage world.

When I told John what I was thinking, he became upset. He was terribly hurt. It was an understandable and natural reaction. He felt that we worked very well together—for many years. Workplace bonds can be strong. He didn't understand why I wanted to leave. I eventually did, though; I left with a small team of people. I took my processor and two other sales-people with me. We landed at three other mortgage companies between leaving John and starting Centennial Lending Group.

John felt that I had left him on a deserted island. In this universe, as we all learn eventually, everything comes back to bite or kiss us. For all my success with John, I realized that I was pretty narrowly skilled from a management standpoint. Beyond what was on a rate sheet, I did not really know how to price loans. I did not know the back end of the operation, nor did I know how loans were sold in the secondary markets. To really learn the business, I had to break away from my mentor and move in a new direction.

Leaving John was hard. He had watched over me and protected me. Loyalty, so important to me, was overshadowed by my need to spread my wings. I had to branch out on my own and learn the business, through and through. The alternative was to remain a salesperson. I knew I wanted more.

Being a salesperson is similar to being a racehorse. The blinders are on and all you care about is the finish line. You are always racing toward that finish. If, however, they forget to put the blinders on, just once, you find you are still running, but you can see all around you. You notice there are options outside that straight line. I left John because I had to grow. I needed to take the blinders off. Leaving him was the only way I could learn everything I needed to about the mortgage industry.

I did not know how to manage a team or run an organiza-tion. Learning to do so would be a tremendous challenge, but

I was ready to take it on. Mastering those skills would ultimately take me to the next level of my career.

Some people do not have that same need or desire to make a change. Some are content with where they are in life. They keep on running the race and they keep hitting their finish line, at their pace, which is good. I just felt something was missing out there that I needed to pursue. Even today, I am always asking myself, "How can I do better?" or "How can we do better?"

"Knowledge is power."

Occasionally, I wonder if I still have blinders on. I think drive is what makes a company or a person excel.

"Is Centennial Lending Group a better place to get a mortgage now than it was three months ago or six months ago or a year ago?" I ask myself. With new procedures in place, we continue to make substantial and positive strides, all in an effort to improve the overall process for our customers. We always look to make things better and we know we must continue to embrace and welcome change. We have to have our fingers on the pulse of the economy, the regulators, and the changes that are happening in the industry.

As a manager, I have learned what works for me. We have recently taken on additional office space. In the process, I sought the advice of a space planner as well as an interior designer. I was able to give them clear instructions on the color scheme I preferred; our colors are brighter than those of most other mortgage companies. Decisions were made about which space would be dedicated to executives and the sales team, and which space would be dedicated to the support team. It all came together once we moved everybody into the new space. It took a lot of preliminary planning, but plans, of course, had to be altered, decisions made on the fly.

It looks perfect now. Our organization has evolved that way. We cannot predict and forecast everything, but we guide ourselves along the way, and we manage to do it well. We do this by staying true to the cultures we have built over the years.

CHAPTER 4

Weeding Out the Duds

Dud /duhd/ *Noun: 1) a thing that fails to work properly;
2) a shell or missile that fails to explode after being fired.*

When I flew the coop and left John Crits in 2006, I took a new position with another mortgage company. My core group and I stayed at this company for two years. During this time, I definitely learned more of the intricacies of operating a mortgage company. I learned how to manage a team of salespeople and staff support personnel, as well. I learned about pricing and how critical it was to any operation. I learned what worked and I also learned what did not work. I learned what I was willing to accept and what was just flat-out unacceptable. I knew I was looking for a company with a certain philosophy. I was determined to work for an organization where I could enjoy some freedom, but also one that would fully support my team and me. I needed an organization that understood how to cater to my customers (borrowers and realtors).

Well, the company I joined was not going to be the right place for me. Some might have said it was a mistake to go there, but I learned a great deal about our industry, both good and bad. I chalked it up to a valuable learning experience. In 2008, I moved to another mortgage company. This company's owner was planning to delegate the actual running of the mortgage company to a new manager, which was the reason I had decided to join that organization. My employment there would prove beneficial to the owner, in that he could now devote his time and energy to the bank side of the operation, which he also owned at the time, although they were completely separate entities. When I evaluated the company, I discovered it had only one employee. She told me it was just her and her radio. "We will do our best to change that!" I remember telling her. I viewed it as a great opportunity, especially from the standpoint of potential growth. The owner considered his company to be the equivalent of a vintage Corvette that had been neglected and was in need of repair. I could relate to this analogy, since I actually knew a little bit about cars.

I decided to take advantage of this new opportunity.

Once again, I brought my team—a processor and two loan officers—along with me.

Unfortunately, I was in for a rude awakening. I was thinking our tarnished Corvette simply needed to be buffed and polished, but that was not quite the case. No engine, no tires, no wheels, and no transmission would be closer to the truth. It needed a total restoration. Early on, we recognized the scope of the work ahead of us, so we rolled up our sleeves and went to work. Moving to a company that was, basically, a shell was a risky proposition, but I knew there would be tremendous satisfaction in resurrecting this company from the ashes. I believed I would be building it for the future, my future. It would become my claim to fame, an accomplishment I would, eventually, be very proud of. It was my vision: building it, overseeing it, and, who knows, maybe one day owning it!

Things went well in the beginning. We had a great crew. We were all dedicated and we had free rein to make decisions. The bigger and more successful we became, the better it looked to the owner. We hired a closer, an underwriter, and two post-closers. We made big strides and significant progress over a short period of time. A little over one year later, the owner viewed the mortgage company as his most valuable investment, and one that he should once again manage. In a sense, you could not blame him. It was his mortgage company and it was now doing exceptionally well. I had added several new investors, secured new warehouse lines, and obtained our full FHA approval, just to cite a few changes. Ironically, the bank side of things, which he was responsible for, was not doing nearly as well.

Somewhere near the end of my second year, the owner decided to take back the mortgage division and head up all operations. Additionally, he would be the sole owner. In essence, he was taking credit for all of our hard work and success. I knew I could not tolerate this. I did not feel our ideologies could find common ground. He started to change the procedures and many of the things I had implemented earlier. He altered things that directly contributed to our success. We were not seeing eye to eye. Without my knowledge, he started to open additional branches, hiring new people to run those branches. Instead of my managing them, I now had direct competitors. When making these hires, he routinely told the incoming managers, "'I will give you the same deal I gave Sue, or better."

In addition, I was not being paid the money I deserved, which had been agreed to. Since I was making more money than I had ever made in my life, he felt I should be happy and content. When I discovered that my checks were not being calculated accurately, I confronted him. "This was not what we agreed to," I told him. He owed me more than $100,000 in commissions that were never paid to me. This bitter lesson made me realize how important it is to be fair and ethical when it comes to compensation. I will always pay our salespeople what they rightfully earn. These were among the lessons that I learned—the hard way.

While dealing with all of this, I was working with a man whom I had trained when he left his entry-level teller position at a bank. He had been my assistant before moving through the ranks to become a loan officer. He pretty much handled all the extra business I could not handle. In essence, he helped me, and in turn, I helped him. After he had worked many years by my side, I considered him more of a partner than a subordinate, and we had gone to this new mortgage company on that basis. We were, in essence, comanaging our team. He did the things he liked to do most and I did the things that I liked to do. It was a good partnership.

We had built quite a team. Everyone had a similar reaction to what was going on at the current company. Privately, we sat down and together assessed the situation. We had our eyes on the door, but we needed to think long and hard about our exit. This was in 2010. I had staff members who needed to provide for their families. If I decided to leave, they would need a home as well. I knew I would eventually open up a mortgage company, so I went looking for a place for all of us to "temporarily" hang our hats. We needed a company that could handle our loans.

We anticipated we would be delivering about $60 million in new business for a six-month period, all the while laying groundwork to start the new company. There was overhead in paying a processor and a closer, but it paled in comparison to the revenue we would be generating. The people at the new lending company understood they would be paying us our commissions for any loans we delivered and closed for them. We agreed this lending company would be responsible for processing the loans that we brought in. It would capitalize on the revenue, and we would have a temporary place to call home. I felt this was a mutually beneficial agreement and there was an understanding that the lending company would not go after the people I brought with me. I was up-front and honest with the new lender and made sure we had a clear understanding that this was only a temporary stopover for us—all of us. Additionally, we had worked with some of the company's people in the past, so there was a degree of comfort since we would be working out of their local branch.

Here is the odd part. I wanted the temporary lending company to be just good enough to get the job done but not too good. I knew I needed to find the perfect nonperfect company for us to move to. There was a method to my madness. I could not risk taking my team to a stellar company. What if my team ended up liking it there? I was concerned, because people tend to settle and become comfortable pretty easily if the results are good. This time, I had to carefully choose a company where my team would really *not* want to stay long term. This way, when I finally opened my own business, they would all come with me. As I said, I was looking for an adequate company, but nothing more. In the end, the company I selected unknowingly handled its role to perfection.

Most of my team hated working there. Each day, someone would ask, "When are we getting out of here?" I ran the risk they might just leave and go elsewhere, but it was a risk I needed to take. I also made it clear to everyone this was not how I wanted things either. As I had anticipated, the people at the lending company encouraged my closer and a loan officer to stay with them, which validated all of my initial concerns. If that company's environment had been better, I could have lost my entire staff to it. Fortunately, that did not happen. Thank goodness for the loyalty of a few of my team!

CHAPTER 5

It Is Always More Than Meets the Eye

People need a roof over their heads. I am of the opinion everybody in America needs a mortgage, but, of course, I am biased. If you rent, you are paying somebody else's mortgage. Wherever you are living, somebody is paying a mortgage or has paid off a mortgage. Would you prefer to pay your own mortgage, or pay someone else's? It is much better to pay your own, in my opinion.

However, the home-buying process carries a cost. When you buy a house and take out a mortgage, it is stressful. Truth and reality hit as cold facts about your finances. Your life in general suddenly becomes an open book to people you have really never met. A loan officer's life is all about sitting down with buyers, getting them to share all the facts and tell their story when, deep down, they do not want to. Making people feel comfortable sharing what they need to share is the key. Home buyers are often reluctant to share information they feel might hurt their chances of getting approved for a mortgage. Often, they think, "I don't want to reveal this or that, so I'll just wait to see if they ask for it."

At the eleventh hour, when they are forced to tell the mortgage company what really happened, it is usually too late in the process. It does not work. I always advise people to come clean with me and air their dirty laundry up front. I will be able to figure out the path of least resistance and it will give me enough time to handle the situation. If something is left out and it happens to be something major, I promise any mortgage company will find out about it eventually. Not revealing everything is a huge issue, and it will only make the borrower's lives and the mortgage process more difficult.

Maybe you are considering buying a townhouse in Philadelphia and you co-own a cottage in the Catskills or up in Maine somewhere. You and your sister own it free and clear. This actually happened with a customer of mine. He did not tell me about the cottage. It may have been an honest oversight, because he seldom if ever went to the cottage. The cottage did not have a lien on it, or a mortgage, so owning it probably felt no different than owning a rowboat or some other posses-sion. A cottage is not a rowboat, however, because taxes and insurance must be paid on it, and that payment is still consid-ered a monthly debt when a new mortgage is being processed.

Even though the taxes and insurance costs on the cottage might total just $200 a month, they could make the borrower's ratios too high and disqualify him for the new mortgage. This is not a fun conversation to have with a borrower: "Sorry, you neglected to tell me you had a house free and clear in Maine because you didn't think it had any significance? However unintentional, the plain fact is you have committed mortgage fraud! And you cannot purchase your new house. This is what the regulations say today." As I said, this is not a fun discussion to have with a potential referral source.

I had another customer who provided me with his tax returns. When I pulled the tax transcripts (we always have to look at third-party tax transcripts), they did not match. I called him. "George, your tax returns are not matching what you filed with the IRS. What is going on?" I asked. He was embarrassed. He had given me the wrong tax return. His accountant had run them once, and then he and his accountant had reviewed them and realized there was a lot of missing information. Changes were made that altered the filing, so the taxes were calculated again and printed out again, but he had provided me with the previous version.

My customer, George, did not realize tax returns are verified by a third party. I knew he had deliberately given me the wrong ones because he thought the huge paper loss he had incurred the previous year would disqualify him. He did not realize this was fraud. We eventually got our hands on the correct returns. In this instance, it ended well.

To be upbeat and optimistic, I often call the home-buying process "the best time of your life." In reality, it is a stressful and difficult time for most people. Other than health concerns or injury, few things put more stress on a relationship than purchasing a house. I have had applicants call and tell me quietly over the phone that if they are not approved when their application comes back from underwriting, that is fine! "In fact, maybe it's for the best," is how a borrower might put it. The borrower may have gotten cold feet, or be intimidated by the mortgage payment or closing costs, and would truly prefer to be turned down. People have gone beyond that and asked me, directly, to decline them, for no reason at all. They forget a seller is involved, and that they signed a legal contract to buy a house. Unfortunately, I cannot decline an application for a mortgage simply because the borrower suddenly has a change of heart. Once a borrower has applied for a mortgage, the mortgage company has an obligation to all parties to access the file and make a decision based on the information given. If borrowers can qualify, we will be able to approve them. If the borrowers cannot qualify, we have to deny the mortgage. Feelings and change of heart cannot enter the equation once a buyer gets this far. So, before putting in an offer, everyone should be prequalified and know the numbers of all the costs involved in purchasing a house. Buyers should be educated and know their options so the issue discussed above is not a concern.

Another customer called me to ask, "When you pull up our credit report and we're sitting with you tonight, is there any way you can keep from showing that I never paid the American Express bill for $10,000? My wife thinks I paid it and she cannot know I didn't." Again, I cannot help you with things like this. We have to disclose everything. All cards have to be out on the table, or else all of us are breaking the law. Everything must be disclosed to all parties.

I had another one of those "bend-the-truth" requests, only this one had a sweet sentiment behind it. A man who was buying a house with his girlfriend had just purchased her diamond engagement ring. There was now a very big charge sitting on his credit card balance. He hadn't proposed to her yet and they had been together a long time. Even though they were buying this house together, she was not expecting a proposal. So, to keep it a surprise, he wanted me to keep quiet about the credit card balance. I told him he was out of luck. "How am I going to pretend that information isn't going on the application?" It was going to be right on the second page of the application where the credit card balances appear, and I would be going over them. There was no way of not seeing it. I told him privately, "You need to propose to her tonight before you get to my office." He did. She said yes!

I have another story on the flip side of the coin. This married couple was buying a house and having to share all personal financial information, perhaps for the very first time. The husband pulled me aside. He wanted to keep one piece of information a secret. It involved child support and alimony he had to pay his previous wife. The only problem was his current wife had no idea her husband had been married previously, let alone had to pay child support and alimony. The alimony payments would soon be finished, but he still had to pay child support until his child turned 18 years of age.

Because of this, I needed his divorce decree. I needed the child support documents and I needed to know how much he was obligated to pay each month. I told him this could no longer be swept under the rug. It was all going on the application, which would be signed again at settlement. And my problem then became, "What if they no longer qualify?" What if I had to tell them they no longer qualified because he had a $700-per-month child support payment? Actually, I only had to tell the husband. He had to tell his wife! (No way was I giving her this information.)

I have had customers who lived from paycheck to paycheck, even though they were top executives at huge firms. Then they left the firm without a new job and could not pay their mortgage for six months. They had great credit. They had a terrific monthly income. Then a report crosses my desk saying they are completely delinquent across the board. This sort of thing happens! Even people you never imagine could become at risk can wind up in a predicament. There is an element of risk involved in buying a house; there is an element of risk involved in dating someone. Risk is associated with almost everything you do, including your job. Our job is to assess the risk and make an educated decision on the likelihood borrowers will make their mortgage payments.

These are stressful times. Sometimes, the process ends in tears. I had a customer who was buying a condo for his soon-to-be ex-wife, his third wife. The husband was contributing a big down payment, but the wife he was divorcing was going to need a mortgage to cover the rest of it. She came in to apply and she was obviously upset. She started to sob in my office because she could not believe she was getting divorced and buying a house by herself. How could this be happening to her?

By now, you know my job is to help people feel comfortable in uncomfortable situations. Sometimes we need to put the business dealings aside and make it all about the person in front of us, the consoling side of things. I listen and offer support. This is, sometimes, part of the job. I end up saying, "It will be okay. I promise." I have to show empathy. I told her, "I too have been through the same thing. I'm divorced. I never thought I would be divorced, but everything happens for a reason." My whole tone had to change and I had to be empathetic and understanding and tell her that she would get through it. "What about my daughter?" she asked. "Will she be scarred for life about this?" I replied, "I'm not sure if she'll be scarred for life, but one thing I do know is that children are resilient. Her father and you will provide for her and be supportive of her."

"When I was going through my own divorce, my children were very young," I told her. (I often talk about my own experiences.) As I spoke, she visibly relaxed in my office. I sensed she felt she could trust me because I truly understood what she was going through. Sometimes we have to deal with emotional issues at an emotional time. This helps us build the relationship and trust with the customer. Being a sharp, competent, effective businessperson is all well and good, but some things take precedence. I may have to switch gears suddenly and become more understanding and compassionate, knowing I am opening up the floodgates. When those gates open . . . in just two minutes you could very well know every unhappy detail of a person's entire life. The hard part is you have to do it tactfully and respectfully. It may not have been what you were expecting when you rolled into work that day. There you are, sitting with someone who is very vulnerable and suddenly she completely breaks down in front of you. "It's okay," I say, "You're going through a really horrible time. I get it." The ability to attend to someone who is truly upset or distressed has helped me to become a better parent, a closer friend, and a stronger businesswoman.

I love developing a stronger bond with my borrowers. I embrace this part of the job rather than run from it. I can be very buttoned up, but I can be very open and available emotionally. There is a time and a place for both. It is my nature to be understanding and compassionate. I feel for all of my customers who are going through tough times. People have shared with me serious problems they are having

"Love what you do!"

with their children. I can honestly say, "I get it." My daughter was born hearing impaired and that reality crushed me at the time. I completely understand the stress of having a child who is about to undergo major surgery. I get the divorce thing. I get how difficult making a major decision in your life can be and the stress it puts on everyone involved. Add the normal stresses of life to the stress of purchasing a house and it is difficult to find a more stressful time. For the loan officer, it is all about bedside manner, which is not something easily taught or, for that matter, understood. I try to tell people I understand what they are enduring and I might even give an example of how I understand. At this point, I have done so many mortgages I think I have seen just about everything. That seasoning is the value I bring to my job. Yet, I am still surprised sometimes.

Not every problem is an easy fix. Sometimes, I just have to say no; there is no solution here. "We've tried everything." A people pleaser by nature, I would love to say yes to everybody. When a mortgage deal does not work out, the realtor is usually the one who is most disappointed, right along with the buyer. Realtors often refer to your past successes. They are quick to remind you that you always seem to come through and you can come through on another one. This kind of pressure weighs heavily on each salesperson. It is even more difficult when you have a realtor who feels you are only as good as your last deal, which at times is beyond your control. This happens all the time. You can see the referral source passing before your eyes. You are never going to get another deal again. Still more pressure. Of course, you want the deal to close and everyone to be happy. Yet this too, at times, is beyond your control.

It is possible to become a victim of your own success. Once, I had a customer who had declared bankruptcy a couple of years earlier and was slow to tell us about it. He did not give us permission to run a credit report before signing an agreement on a house purchase. I saw the bankruptcy as soon as I ran the credit report. I racked my brain day and night, but we could not get around it, especially since we were not aware of the problem prior to writing the offer. If you have had a bankruptcy within three years, it cannot be removed from your credit report. It is just not going to happen. A bankruptcy has to be discharged for two years for an FHA loan, and seven for a conventional loan, to have a chance. You must have reestablished new debt and not had another late payment on anything. When realtors or borrowers bring situations like this to me, I have to be careful to make sure they understand the results are out of my control. I was not the one who decided to declare bankruptcy.

Being the fix-it person and having a can-do attitude is great, but you have to send a clear message to customers that they have responsibilities as well. Owning a house is a major commitment and responsibility. The commitment begins when you apply for the mortgage. Obviously, we all have a common goal. We want the deal to work. Most mortgage professionals are take-charge, take-control people. They want everything to go smoothly and will do anything within reason to make sure it does. The more processes and procedures you have in place, the smoother the transaction. The more organized the borrower is, the smoother the transaction. The more everyone communicates effectively, the smoother the transaction.

In the mortgage business, you have to worry about your referral source as much, if not more, than the relationship with your customer. For the loan officer, there are considerations beyond the deal you are working on at the time. You have to think about the future deals you could be jeopardizing if the transaction is not perfectly orchestrated, especially at the settlement. When you buy a house, generally, you like your realtor, and you like your loan officer, but you may never know if they like each other. Their relationship seems chummy, but it may actually be tenuous. There are times when a realtor, in a squeeze, has been known to lay down a threat, as in, "Fix this or I will never use you again." I tell my loan officers, "When you hear a threat, it's serious." In the eyes of the realtor, you are only as good as your last deal. This is really hard to swallow if you have had a long-term relationship with someone. You may be looking at a realtor who has given you 60 deals over the last four years, and yet he is saying he may not be able to give you any more business if this deal does not go through. You always need to keep in the back of your mind this is a stressful time for them too.

We have all had to deal with this at some time or another. I have one story that always reminds me not to cut off my nose to spite my face. I had a realtor who handed out my business card to customers and recommended me as his "preferred" mortgage person. One day, after years of working together, he decided to hand out two cards, mine and a competitor's card. He must have felt that I had let him down, or was not paying enough attention to him, or something else that was relatively minor, such as not calling a buyer back fast enough. Whatever it was, it was enough for him to decide he was going to start handing out two business cards.

I found this out and I approached him. "Did I understand you correctly? You're giving your customers two cards now? I don't have any problem with buyers going out and finding mortgage people to work with. But when you refer me, knowing the relationship we have, I think that you should just hand them my card, because I've never let you down." He said, "Well, Sue, I've decided that I'm going to give your card out and I'm going to give a competitor's card out, as well."

I knew if I went up against this other mortgage officer on any given day, I could compete with him easily in service and price. However, I said, regretfully, "If you're going to give their card out, then don't bother giving my card out." This realtor, the one I had worked with for all those years, did just that. He took me at my word. From then on, he gave only my competitor's card out to buyers. So, this was Sue letting her competitiveness, and maybe her ego, get firmly in the way. I was cutting off my nose to spite my face.

This happened probably over ten years ago. Over time, I ended up doing a lot of business with his business partner. He would say, "I only use Sue. She never lets me down." That was his partner's mantra. I loved doing business with him. We had a fantastic working relationship. It is great when you have a realtor or any referral partner who becomes your true raving fan. It helps both of you develop your business platform and work together as a team. I have been lucky enough to have had many of those relationships in the last two decades and I value those partnerships even as my positions have evolved. I treasure the friendships that have come about over time.

People make decisions. They may have to deal with the consequences of those decisions. You can create problems for yourself that will have to be solved eventually, or you can make sound decisions that, in the long run, will help you be successful. Even when it works out in a positive way, your success may still come with a price. Not everyone may see it, but you will.

I am not at home when my children come home from school. I am not at every football, baseball, and basketball game, but I try to get to as many of my children's games as possible. Sometimes my friends do not hear from me for a week or two at a time. My relationship with my significant other has a tricky aspect: We live in different states, three hours apart. He does not see how hard I work during the week, yet he does understand. My friends all know I love them, but they do not talk to me every day. My job is Centennial Lending Group and my bigger job is being the best mom I can be for my two children. Just like those folks taking out a mortgage, sometimes there is more to the story. There is always more than meets the eye.

The reality is I, like everyone, have a family to support. I need to earn what it takes to give my family security. There have been weeks when I worked 60 hours. Recently, I had a long discussion with my daughter, Allyson, about her tutoring, which she was trying to avoid. I told her she needed to work in school the way I worked at my company. I work hard for the lifestyle she and her brother enjoy. That includes her tutors. Her end of the bargain is to attend the sessions and do the assigned work. I told her she had to be as dedicated to her schoolwork as I was to my work. After this conversation, she now seems to have a better understanding of going the extra step. It was a big conversation about how much everything costs and she is now mature enough to understand everything comes at a price.

A few weeks ago, her brother, Drew, stayed home from school because he was not feeling well. When he went to play his Xbox, he discovered I had removed the cord from the television. I told him all decisions have consequences. He had decided he did not feel well and was not going to school. This was a ramification of that decision. As far as I was concerned, he was not going to stay home to have fun, especially if he was not feeling well. These are fundamental lessons. I think it is vital to learn these valuable lessons, even at age 11 and age 13.

My children can clearly see the process of working for what they want, at least most of the time. Drew, my son, is going into eighth grade. The entrance requirements for the high school he wants to attend are stringent and will soon affect him. The school requires an entrance test, good grades, and an interview. Prospective students have to take a tour of the school. It is all taken very seriously, which, in turn, sets the bar for him to do well so he can move on to college. We are preparing carefully, well in advance. We are used to teaching this to our children, so why would we not do the same thing for our company? I am preparing my child for college, which is six years from now. This correlation also applies to my company. We need to remain focused, and keep our sights set on our goals, to have a clear direction going forward for the next six years, and the next six years after that and into the future.

CHAPTER 6

Referrals, Referrals, Referrals

When you bought your house, did the loan officer come to your settlement? For me, this is the sign of someone who is committed and serious about both the business and his career. Good loan officers value future referrals and make it a point to build their business. Most of the really good loan officers attend their settlements. That is when they really get to shine and say, "We did a great job." Conversely, if they do not attend the settlement, they do not care enough about their borrowers or future business. Attending their own settlements shows they are confident about their company and about themselves. It also shows they want to see the process through to the end and appreciate referrals as a consequence of their efforts. I want borrowers to think the world of me and believe that no other mortgage consultant could do as good a job. I need to be sure I am going to become their mortgage consultant for life. So, when anyone mentions applying for a mortgage, my name and company comes right out of my past customers' mouths.

I was lucky in a weird way when I entered the mortgage business. Rates were sky high, around 9 percent. Telling people I could get them a great rate, when I knew how high the rates were, was a hard sell. Selling rates at 9 percent was difficult but taught me if I could sell rates at 9 percent, I could sell them at any percent. After I built my original base of customers, rates began falling. As the 1990s rolled on, mortgage rates kept ticking down, down, down. People with mortgages at higher or adjustable rates wanted to refinance to a lower rate, which was great for me. My belief in building a good customer relationship was validated as I built on these relationships and generated repeat business from those same customers. Once again, trust and good service allowed my past customers to return to me, as their mortgage consultant.

Over the years, as interest rates plummeted, my customers would come back to me two, three, or even four times, allowing me to develop a huge past-customer database. These customers started with me when I was 25 years old and went right through into my 30s and 40s. I had one customer who knew me when I started in the business. He first applied with me before my marriage, again when I had my first child, again when I had my second child, and then, yes, a fourth application when I went through my divorce. He watched me go through the most important phases of my life, and I watched him doing the same. I am now very close to a whole generation of people whose mortgages I have worked on through the years. We have all grown up together. I guess we will grow old together, which is nice—lots of good, lasting relationships over time.

One customer has referred many of his relatives, friends, and his employees to me. The biggest thank-you one could possibly receive is a referral. I probably have 5,000 past customers and I love their referrals. It never gets old. I make sure to tell those who compliment me that the best compliment they can give is to refer their friends to me. People sometimes need to hear you ask for the referral. They may not know just how critical it is to business. I make a point of spelling it out.

"Ask for the future business and ask for the referral."

In my view, the referral system is critical. It is what makes the business world go round. My dad has many friends who are all professionals and they all help each other. They do not work with those who have the best price; they work with those they trust. It is a relationship that is built over time. Today, when customers are applying for mortgages, I tell them to find someone who gives them a good, secure feeling; to work with someone they trust, not someone who has the best interest rate. Fees and interest rates are similar for everyone. It is all about whom you trust and with whom you can build a lasting relationship. You want someone who will remember you and your situation, someone who will answer your questions at any time, and especially, someone to be there for you when it comes to your next important purchase.

Trust means making sure you understand what your customer needs. I often ask a borrower, "In a perfect world, what would your mortgage payment look like?" If the borrower names an amount of $2,000, I work the loan up so it comes as close to $2,000 as possible and the borrower is usually comfortable with this approach. I am not being asked what the interest rate is. I am not being asked what the fees are on the product. Borrowers trust me because I listen to them and give them exactly what they are looking for in a payment. They are saying they are comfortable with the mortgage payment we discussed. When you buy a house, you may think you will be in that house forever. You think it is a once-and-done deal, but you do not know what the future holds. You do not know if you will have to refinance or if you will have more children. You may have to upgrade to something larger. You may get divorced, or, as you get older, you may have to sell the house. You may think you are going to get only one mortgage in your lifetime, but realistically, you may get five or six. Do you really want to use a new mortgage person every single time?

In my experience, some people today seem to miss this relationship-building experience. Do you change doctors every year? Do you ask different lawyers to do all your estate planning? You have a financial advisor who has guided you in your financial planning and now you're going to switch to a new one because his fee is lower? That probably is not in your best interest. Do you shop for a brain surgeon on the Internet and make sure her price is the cheapest around? It is no different with your mortgage person. It is no fun to be stripped naked and tell a stranger everything about your finances. When my past customers call me, I have most of their information in a database. The file just needs some updating, and it all goes smoothly. They do not have to explain everything to me, because I have already seen it. I already know about their skeletons. I treat them as the trusted, priceless customers they are to me.

What I see as fundamental to both my and my company's success is treating every single mortgage loan as something much bigger than a mere loan. With each transaction, I am building for the future, toward making a customer one for life. It should roll off my customers' lips: "If you need a mortgage, call Sue." I might be the CEO of a company, but I am going to make sure my customers are taken care of. They can call me anytime should anything go wrong and that is exactly what they do.

Available, Accessible, Always!

People, sometimes, do not understand the importance of maintaining relationships and how they can benefit from them. Some do not recognize the value of above-and-beyond service. However, when they are in a bind, it suddenly resonates with them. When Hurricane Sandy hit the Northeast, and all those homes were flooded and wind damaged, we were inundated with phone calls. In several cases, homeowners for whom we had handled mortgages called our loan officers. We immediately provided assistance and sent contractors directly to those who needed them. We went above and beyond in the service we provided during an awful episode. It is not glitz and glitter all the time. Our business has plenty of challenging situations. My definition of excellence is consistently going above and beyond while setting and managing all expectations.

I stress to our salespeople the importance of managing expectations. If your customers do not expect the world but you deliver it, they will be really happy with you. That is so important. Do not tell somebody you are going to get back to him today and then make him wait until the next day. Tell him it is going to take three days to receive a commitment. Then, when he receives it the next day, he's excited. You overdelivered! We all need to pursue a reputation for overdelivering. This also maintains our integrity. We are building on trust.

As CEO, I occasionally am asked to pinch hit. One of the loan officers came to me a while back, during a very busy period, and asked if I could handle a settlement for her. She had several deals closing all at once. Truly, it was a great problem, but it had to be handled. At our company, we strongly advise the loan officers to attend closings. If there is a conflict, they need to find someone to cover for them. When she asked me, I was more than happy to do it. She gave me the office location and I went there. Before I left, I went through all of the documentation. The borrower's name was familiar to me. When I arrived at the office, it turned out I had completed a purchase and a refinance mortgage for him. He came back to Centennial

Lending Group through the recommendation of his realtor. He said to me, "You were phenomenal the first two times. That's why I knew when I was referred to your company everything would go smoothly."

I remembered he and his wife were teachers and, as luck would have it, I was able to go over the paperwork with them, and they expressed their gratitude. I thanked them for their loyalty. That is, basically, the story of my career. It also showed me referrals could be institutionalized. This customer shifted his respect and admiration for *me* and applied it to my *company*. That is a really great feeling and a huge accomplishment!

Of course, we worked hard to deliver the service to earn each of those referrals. Of all the statements I could make about our customer service, none of them holds more weight than this one. I have never failed to get the money to the settlement table—on time! Not many mortgage companies can say that today.

Everything matters in business. However, one thing always matters more than anything else: Delivering the money to the settlement table on time is where the rubber hits the road when it comes to mortgage lending. Not delivering the money to the table is pure failure. Everybody in the room starts looking for a hole to crawl into. I have received many a phone call from people in that very situation, although, thankfully, none of them work at Centennial Lending Group. These are the 911 calls of our industry, code-blue emergencies. A nervous couple sitting at the settlement table and being told their mortgage is not approved or something went terribly wrong is a nightmare scenario. When I worked in a RE/MAX office, it was the norm for an agent to walk in and say, "The money's not here. How fast can you close a loan? The funds aren't going to be here until tomorrow," and I'd say, "I can close it this afternoon. Just get me the package." We would take the application, get it underwritten, and close it. Literally, it would happen within hours. This is what I am talking about: unmatched and unheard of service! Yet, this was years ago when you could immediately close a loan.

I did this all the time. The buyers would sign the necessary papers and I would send their package over to my office, making sure I had their paystubs, their W-2s, and their bank statements. I would order a quick appraisal. My appraiser would go out on the spot. Back then, it was possible. We would then order the funds electronically or bring the check. Somebody would drive the paperwork to settlement, and before you knew it, we would close the purchase. The realtor would be thrilled and, once again, we would be the shining stars. The buyers would be so appreciative and thankful. They would be able to move into their new home.

Closing so quickly is not allowed anymore. There is now a seven-day waiting period, per regulations. But when it was possible, we took such pride in being able to get the job done, especially when another company had failed to do so. The other company had overpromised and underdelivered. That was its problem. Its reputation was on the line, just as mine would have been if I had failed to get the funds to the settlement table on time. Fortunately, that has never happened to me. The bottom line is if I want those referrals to continue to find their way to Centennial Lending Group, we have to deliver each and every time, without fail.

CHAPTER 7

· ·

No More Rabbits in the Hat

first sensed trouble brewing in the mortgage industry sometime around 2006 or 2007. Common sense was out the window. I think of those years as my "in-between period." I had left my longtime employer, Philadelphia Financial, and Centennial Lending Group would not be launched until 2010. During this time, I worked at several different companies. I kept doing what had worked so well in the past. As I learned to overdeliver to my customers, I also learned to overdocument mortgage applications. The more information I secured from the borrowers, the fewer items we would have to ask for later. With this philosophy, everything went more smoothly.

Management suddenly told processors to discard pertinent information. They would tell us we no longer needed it. This was very confusing, and not what I had been taught. I asked management, "Why is this not necessary?" I felt we needed to archive all information we had gathered on a file, as a precautionary measure, just in case we got called on it. They said we simply didn't need any of that stuff anymore. "Well, we have it, so we may as well keep it in the file," I replied. That did not go over well.

At times, I would say, "I can't believe we can do this mortgage. How can we do a mortgage for somebody who has a 64 back-end ratio [64 percent of the borrower's income went toward their mortgage and debt]? After you take out taxes, they can't afford groceries. How can we give them a mortgage?" I spoke frankly to borrowers, telling them, in my professional opinion, they could not afford the house they were about to buy. Their response, often, was to go down the road and get the mortgage from someone who would readily do it for them. There were times I put them into a mortgage they barely qualified for; they were approved via the automated system, despite my concerns. Some conscientious borrowers did pay their mortgages and figured out a way to afford them, but many did not. As I said earlier, I have never closed a bad mortgage in my entire career. I have never done a negative-amortization mortgage or issued one with a prepayment-penalty, and yet, for a while, I was embarrassed to say what I did for a living. I could not control what was happening in the rest of the mortgage industry. Sometimes, things are just beyond your control.

I sensed there would be a reckoning, and when it came, it would not be pretty. I also thought it would not have as great an impact on me as it might on others. It would be disastrous for mortgage companies that were guilty of those crazy loans. I went about my business with the expectation those practices would have to end sometime, and they did, as we all know. Contrary to my prediction, everyone was affected, including me. I started wondering if mortgages were becoming a thing of the past. The fact is they were—and are—not over, but sweeping, necessary changes would eventually overhaul our industry. We now tell prospective home buyers—who we believe can afford a mortgage payment—that Fannie Mae and Freddie Mac, the government agencies insuring the loans, will not allow them to take on a loan of the size they are requesting. They will have to set their sights on a less expensive home— that is, if they can get a mortgage at all. Mortgages have to fit into such a specific box. Sometimes, even a perfect buyer, for one reason or another, may have an issue obtaining one.

However, I soon discovered there are things we can control. For instance, I advise all my loan officers to obtain tax returns. Some items, such as unreimbursed business expenses, can kill a loan, and will only be discovered by looking at their tax returns. Any mortgage company will have an issue with unreimbursed business expenses, but all too often, it happens at the very end of the process. At my company, we like to address any potential problems or issues at the very beginning. Experience tells me the longer a problem lingers, the bigger it gets, especially as the settlement date moves closer.

In the old days, corners were cut to streamline the process for the customer. However, history has taught us such a process was easily abused, or taken to extremes by too many. Unfortunately, none of it benefitted the customer as it was intended to. In hindsight, it had a devastating effect on the market and the global economy.

While trying to reform the mortgage business, the regulators went from one extreme to another. Well-intended rules have been put into place that effectively handcuff the loan officer from looking out for the borrower's best interest.

The good faith estimate of settlement charge, which must be given to every borrower, is an example of such a rule. It cannot be changed within three days of the closing. Many times in the past, when we were at the settlement table, we might say, "You're short $1,000 to close. We'll make the loan amount $1,000 higher, or we'll give the lender credit for $1,000 dollars," and all was fine. Now there is no easy fix for any of these things without pushing the settlement back three days. Everyone involved in the process is hurt when the settlement is pushed back. Although circumstances like that are out of our control, we can do a lot to make sure borrowers are aware of such potential problems. The industry abounds with examples such as this. Imagine you are purchasing a house, and during the walk-through something changes. You see carpet stains you were unaware of during the home inspection. If there were a seller credit for the maximum amount, this additional carpet cleaning expense could not be absorbed or accounted for at settlement. You cannot reduce the selling price or change the loan amount. You cannot alter the closing costs or modify the seller credit. At this point, nothing can be changed. To make any changes, all parties must wait three business days and a whole new good faith estimate must be prepared and signed, which is called a change of circumstance.

Who is enforcing all of these new regulations? The Consumer Protection Finance Bureau, along with each state's department of banking. Meanwhile, a lot of mortgage professionals are leaving mortgage companies and migrating to banks, because the regulations are less stringent. Large nationwide banks, for instance, do not have to follow the same loan officer licensing rules as a mortgage banker does. We have to go through multiple certifications and background checks, and we have to score high enough on each test to avoid jeopardizing our business license. After you've invested 10 to 15 years in a career, can you imagine being dealt that news? Some are unable to pass and have to change careers. I scored a 92 on the first major licensing test, but I was a little nervous going into it because I hadn't taken a test for 15 years. There are experienced loan officers who are desperately trying to pass this test

"Try to cover everything that might go wrong up-front and make your buyers and realtors aware of the regulations you are working with at the time."

but cannot because they have not taken a test in well over 30 years, let alone a test on a computer.

As a result, a certain percentage of loan officers who cannot pass the test opt out of the industry. It also forces mortgage professionals to work at the bigger banks. This hurts our industry, the correspondent lending industry, because those who work at bigger banks are paid less. Typically, they are not licensed, and often, they do not rise to the same level of professionalism to be found at a company such as ours. So, what can we control? We can make sure our customers know we are held to a higher standard. I am always encouraging our loan officers to take the negative out and make things work for our customers.

Where does this leave the mortgage industry? Our hope is it leaves us in a better place. We have to deal with greater regulation and more reporting on a daily basis, and this has made it more costly to do business. I believe, however, licensing has brought a sense of professionalism back to the industry.

As for pulling rabbits out of my hat, borrowers need to be as up-front as possible about their personal situations. If you get $2,000 from a relative and plan to deposit it in your bank account the week before closing, please let someone know. If the mortgage company does not know about it until the week of closing, many questions will have to be addressed and answered at the eleventh hour. Going forward, everything must be fully documented and explained. What has changed is there are no more magic acts or tricks up our sleeves, no more rabbits for us to pull out of our hats.

CHAPTER 8

Breaking Up Is Hard to Do

The years between leaving my mentor and being self-employed at Centennial Lending Group were professionally and personally challenging. In my view, many practices were not only inappropriate but also not entirely above board. Often, I felt our support team was treated abysmally by others who held top positions. I dedicated myself to the mortgage industry and I enjoyed working. Although I was making a good living, I had reached a crossroads, questioning not only where my career was going but also my overall happiness. When I looked around, I realized I had no suitable place to hang my hat or to call home.

I went to see my father one day. "Dad, I have no idea which company to go to next." He said, "Are we going to go through this all over again?" He had followed my career from the beginning and watched me not only build two operations, but also run them. "Why not just open your own company?" It was not that simple, I explained to him; in fact, it was a daunting proposition. "Why?" he asked. I told him it would take a lot of money. "How much?" he asked. "Somewhere between $2.5 and $3 million dollars to do it right," I said. There would be enormous risk, especially in light of the national economic situation we were in at the time. My dad took it all in and told me if I decided to start my own company, he would support me and help me to figure out where to get the necessary funding.

Most people thought I had picked the worst possible time to start a mortgage company. I, however, did not see it that way. My biggest advantage was starting my career when interest rates were incredibly high. Everyone who bought homes back then became increasingly unnerved by the astronomical rates they paid monthly. During that period, there were very few, if any, refinance transactions to rely on. But people still moved, houses were still bought and sold, and mortgages were still being approved to close. I figured if I could sell mortgages during such a volatile period, I could make it through almost anything. In other words, I could start a company in 2010, during the worst of economic times along with the worst mortgage market ever, and I could succeed at it. At least rates were low, right? Plus, I was starting with a clean slate. Those factors were the silver lining. I also had a great team I thought would join me.

We were able to create Centennial Lending Group because we had a stellar book of business and we did things the right way. Still, it was hard with the zillion new regulations we were up against in our industry because of what had taken place back in 2008.

While working at my office, I spent considerable time trying to figure out who was on board with my opening up a company. Who would remain loyal? I had my partner and I had my best friend from high school. Both were going to be loan officers at the new venture. Kristi and Joy assured me they were coming as part of the staff. We started working toward our common goal in early 2010. It took about six months to get the company up and running. Raising the $2.5 million and figuring out staffing details were my first priorities. (Adding to the already tremendous pressure, I was 100 percent responsible for supporting my family.) In early 2010 my partner and I set out to raise the $2.5 million. He and I disagreed on whether we should be mortgage bankers or just brokers.

In my opinion, to do it correctly, it takes more than $2 million to become a mortgage banker and substantially less to become a mortgage broker. While the capital requirement is less for a broker, the tradeoff is the broker does not have nearly as much control. I felt control would be vital to our business. It was important to me to be a correspondent lender, for a couple of reasons. One, it gave me more control, and two, I had always done business this way. We also agreed all of the main parties needed to invest some money or have "skin in the game." We thought all our investors were in agreement.

Since he was putting up "sweat" equity, my partner felt he should not have to put up founder's capital, which immediately put him at odds with the other investors. Meanwhile, he had been working on a name and a logo for our company without my knowledge. This was just one area of contention. We were throwing ideas around, but I did not like the name he had picked or the logo, for that matter. It happened to be my birthday when he presented his ideas. He viewed his choosing our company name and logo as a birthday gift. I was none too impressed and I remember responding quite negatively. I may have offended him, but I was offended too.

I started to get an uneasy feeling. Over time, I have learned to trust those gut feelings. We had to get our fingerprints taken and make other legal preparations, such as getting our bond and insurance documents. To do this, we had to go to New Jersey. My phone rang as I was sitting in my car with him. It was my dad. He had just been informed that my partner was in contact with the same insurance agent who was giving us our bond for the new company. Apparently, he had inquired about getting a bond for opening a separate mortgage broker company. Clearly, this indicated the direction he wanted for the new company. I hung up the phone and thought about what to do next.

While heading down the New Jersey Turnpike on the way back to our office, I said, "You know, I got a really peculiar phone call. I know we had a disagreement about the name and logo. I know you said you weren't 100 percent sure you wanted to be my partner, but you said you would be a loan officer at the new company. Have things changed?" He said, "Definitely not. I don't know if it's going to be for six months or a year, but I have every intention of being with you." I said, "That's really strange, because I just received a phone call from my dad. He said he just hung up with the insurance agent who said you were applying to get your broker's insurance. So why would you need broker's insurance if you were just going to originate for me?" Immediately, I could tell he was upset because I had found this out.

The next weekend, I went away to Virginia. My significant other lives there during the week. David has been my rock over the last five years, not to mention the love of my life. We met in college. He knows me better than he knows anyone. He understands me and we work well together as a couple, even though we took a decade-long break from each other. Usually, David comes home to Pennsylvania on the weekends, but this time, I went to Virginia for a much-needed weekend away, which I do from time to time.

When I came back, there was something different about our office. I went to my partner's side of the office and looked around. I just had a strange feeling. Papers and files were on the desk. The business cards were in the normal place. His computer screen and keyboard looked normal. Then my eyes somehow wandered to the floor. The tower to the computer was gone.

I immediately knew what was going on, but I called him anyway. I said, "Why do you have the tower to your computer?" He said, "Oh, because I was going to work from home a little."

Then I started to sift through his desk and open his drawers, whereupon I realized the papers in the files were all blanks. The business cards in his business card holder were not his. It was reminiscent of teenagers sneaking out in the middle of the night and putting pillows in their bed to fool their parents.

And so it goes. That was the end of that relationship.

We had developed a solid working relationship over a ten-year period. Given his ambitions, I knew if I did not make him an equal partner at some point in time, he would eventually move on and do his own thing anyway. Lessons such as these come full circle. It was not unlike what I had done when I left John. I had gradually promoted him to higher levels until our status was pretty much equal, and I thought that would be enough. It obviously was not. He had decided he needed to move on to start his own company.

I was upset and, truth be told, I was upset for a while. As time passed, and I thought about it more, I saw the situation mirrored my leaving John and I got over it. I think it is great he started his own company and I wish him nothing but the best. He and I both had to break away from our mentors, and we did just that. Losing my partner actually helped me progress on my own career path. I had to take a big step back and evaluate what I was doing and how I was going about accomplishing it. I am positive the growth of my company would not have been nearly as dynamic had it not been for that chain of events.

Now, I had to go to my investors and tell them an integral part of the package I had sold to them was gone. They handled the news well and felt it offered an opportunity to modify our business plan. I reworked my plan and the image of the company itself, and changed the name to Centennial Lending Group. I knew I needed someone with a strong accounting and systems background. Thankfully, one of my investors had the perfect CFO candidate for me.

I met with Steven Winokur, and we clicked within minutes. Not only did we work out a job offer, but he also wanted to invest in the company. It was a win-win for both of us. Now I could work on my business plan and go back to figuring out a company name and seeing to the details of incorporating, all while doing business at the temporary company. The good news was I still had my sales force securely in place—a lifelong friend (not Hasty) and me, side by side. "Life is good," I thought.

My lifelong friend (at the time) had worked on and off with me my entire adult working career. I was thrilled she was on board with our plan. I never kept the plan a secret from her, and she had never said anything to the contrary. When we were getting close to opening up the company, however, she too decided not to come with me. Apparently, she did not want my being the boss to affect our friendship. Ironically, that is exactly what happened. She was not just a business acquaintance or just a friend; she was the godmother of my children. When she told me she was not coming after all, I was completely devastated. I cried for days every time I thought of her not coming to the new company. This was mostly because I felt so let down and hurt. I had a difficult time moving away from those feelings, even years later. Once again, I had to reassess the situation. I had to tell my investors that my original plan of bringing two experienced loan officers to the company and originating $120 million worth of business was gone as well. We were now down to only me and what I could produce, which would amount to approximately $40 million or $50 million worth of business. It was still a sizable volume for one person, but it certainly was not what I had originally proposed. Although my processor said she was still coming with me, and my closer acknowledged she was still coming with me, after I discovered my partner of ten years and my lifelong friend were not coming with me, all bets were off. I was unsure of everyone.

I remember saying to the investors, "All I can promise you, at this point, is me." This was the only thing I could guarantee. I said, "I'm going to work really hard to make this company a success. Failure is just not an option." Part of me felt really knocked down, but I was still going forward with a strong, positive attitude. All of my investors saw my commitment and stood behind me. That meant everything to me. The people who had invested in me, and the company, fully supported me. They trusted me to grow the business, regardless of the obstacles in my path, even ones I never dreamed of.

When I decided to launch Centennial Lending Group, I felt it was important to go back and rebuild any bridges I had burned years earlier. This meant having a frank conversation with John Crits. He and I had not spoken for several years. John and his partner decided to part ways and sell the company. He got out before everything went down the tubes with the entire industry. When that sale was consummated, he satisfied his noncompete clause. Then he went to work at one of the big national companies. However, it was not what he was used to and he decided to get out of the mortgage business altogether.

John and I had grown apart because I felt I had to take the blinders off and do it on my own. This was after working together for 16 years. It was important for me to meet with him and tell him I was sorry about the way I had left him. Both of us felt I had left him on an island, all by himself. I had run into him a couple of times, chance meetings that were very awkward. Then I decided I needed to telephone him and ask to meet so we could talk. We met for a cocktail, and I said, "I just wanted to thank you for everything you've done for me over my career. I plan on opening up a mortgage company and I want to be sure there is no ill will between us. I miss your friendship and I'd like to get back to being friends."

He seemed glad to hear this from me. I know he appreciated my calling, and he thanked me for my apology. We both left the meeting feeling better about our friendship. A few months later, I needed a sales manager at Centennial Lending Group. John was the first and only person I thought of to fill this position. I picked up the phone and I told him he was the best in the business, and I did not even have a second choice. I wanted him on our executive team. Not that I gave him a choice, but he said yes after I asked three times. So, now he is our national sales manager and things have come full circle. The person who hired me into the mortgage business ended up coming out of retirement to work with me and help build this new venture. I think John would tell you he is having more fun today than he did when he owned and operated his own company. I will tell you I am so glad he is here with me. I know John will always have my back, which is reassuring and important to me.

John is an outstanding sales and recruiting manager. Each and every day I give thanks for our fantastic management team. Everyone at Centennial Lending Group was handpicked from different companies and walks of life. All of them are at different stages in their life, which I find phenomenal.

For all the satisfaction of recruiting John as sales manager and the satisfaction of recruiting our other managers, I am still disappointed not to have the people I thought would originally come with me, but I am pretty sure everything happens for a reason. Who is to say that my company would be as dynamic as it is today if everything had moved forward as planned initially? We had made three moves together, but they were not going to be part of my new business. While, at the time, it was a huge blow, it was also a true learning experience. I have put a lot of energy and resources into building this team, and I now know one person will not make or break this company.

"Trust your instincts!"

We make offers and some say yes and some say no. Either way, I know we will be just fine. When I did not get the underwriter I wanted, I just kept moving forward and found someone I thought was even better. When it comes to staffing, everything happens for a reason.

I had another problem during this start-up time: Regulations prohibit you from working for two mortgage companies at the same time. I had to have my license at the new company to open it for business. However, I still had to do business with the temporary company. I had to provide for my family. I could not just stop doing mortgages. So, I could not hang my license at the new company—yet. The solution was to have my dad go to the 20-hour class, learn all the material, get fingerprinted twice, take two different tests, and have the whole company opened in his name with his new license.

Here was my father, in his 60s, a nervous wreck because he was suddenly being asked to take a national test and a state test, and he had never sold a mortgage in his entire life. In effect, my whole career and the company were riding on my father's passing two tests—which he did with flying colors! Of course, now it is funny, because Dad still maintains his license. He is one of those people who will keep a useful asset, even if he is not actively using it. He figures as long as he worked so hard to get it, he might as well keep it. It was my company, but everything went into my father's name because it had to be someone I could trust. As soon as I resigned, or was cut loose by the temporary mortgage company, everything would be switched over to me, but in hindsight, that was a tricky transition.

I was honest when I made my last move and the company staff knew I was going to leave at some point. They liked my business, but they kept their eyes on me the entire time. It turned out they were looking to see if my website was going live. That would be the telltale sign, indicating we had launched and were operating the business.

One day, they saw I had tested my website. They called and asked me if I had opened my new business. I said no, and they promptly told me my website had just popped up on Google, so I must be open. I told them we were just testing the system. They did not care, however. They now considered me to be a competitor. They terminated our relationship in October 2010. The timing was almost perfect, because Steven and another staff member had already begun working at Centennial Lending Group. We were safely ensconced in our temporary office space; our future office was under construction. We did not choose the timing, but, miraculously, it worked out just fine.

When we started, I said I would never hire any loan officers until I knew our systems and procedures worked flawlessly for me. It had to be a well-oiled machine before I would hire any salespeople. Remember, I was opening this company so things could be done my way. I was confident my approach was best for all of us, but I had to be assured everything worked correctly. So it was just me and my loans. My loans were the guinea pigs. Only I could take on that risk, initially. I would never have asked any other loan officer to do so. So, effective October 2010, we started operations at Centennial Lending Group. It was just my core group of people and me at *my* company, Centennial Lending Group. It had a nice ring to it.

That is how it all started many years ago. We were able to get all the processes, procedures and quality controls in place. We created systems and we tested them religiously. If something did not work, we changed it immediately. Our volume was not huge, so we looked at every detail, every step of the way, for every loan, until we were comfortable. With John now on board and everything working as a well-oiled machine, we hired our first loan officer in February, and our second and third loan officers shortly thereafter.

Today, years later, Centennial Lending Group has more than 45 employees. Some people who joined us did not work out, but I am pretty sure they are not having as much fun as they did when they were here. I suspect they thought the grass was greener in other mortgage pastures. The truth is the grass is seldom greener, but if they were not content or happy working at Centennial Lending Group, then the best thing for them was to simply be happy—elsewhere.

CHAPTER 9

Love at First Sight?

Although I had a very clear vision of how Centennial Lending Group would operate, I had no idea what being a CEO would be like. In so many ways, it is better than I expected. I have kept my vision for the company, and I have been figuring out the CEO part on the fly.

What I wanted for the company was quite simple. Centennial Lending Group would have cream-of-the-crop loan officers who did things the right way. They should feel completely supported, do well for themselves and their families, and help to keep office morale as positive as possible.

We have processing, closing, and underwriting all in one location. I try to give our loan officers everything they need, from stellar support to pricing to marketing to branding to top-notch underwriting, right through processing and closing. All should be conveniently situated in one place where staff members have access to whatever they need, whenever they need it. We are positioned for everything, and have a full administrative staff. A real person answers our phones. Our staff is smart, and the collective attitude is "no problem is too big for us to handle." If there is a problem, we come up with a solution. Rarely is the answer no, even if other companies have said no. We are fast, efficient, and professional, and we do it with style and class. Put that all together and you have what we call Centennial Lending Group's special sauce.

I will go back to what I said earlier in this book: applying for a mortgage puts people in a sensitive position. Customers of any business want to trust the people they hire, but mortgage applicants have a special need for trust. They need to know they are valued. So, as I look around my company, I need to keep seeing good, smart, trustworthy people with solid judgment and ethics. Customers will give you all of their information as long as they feel they can trust whom they are giving it to. I stress to our staff the need to reach out to people in person, not by e-mail or text. You have to pick up the phone and talk to people. And when you are talking, you have to make your customers understand why you need the requested information and make them feel comfortable giving it to you.

When no one reaches out to you or picks up the phone to call you, it feels like sitting in a restaurant, neglected, ignored, with no one coming to your table. You wait and wait until, eventually, you feel like walking out. If, however, someone comes up to you and says, "Your filet mignon fell on the floor and we have to make you another one and that's going to take a while," well, at least you know the situation. Silence is what really breaks trust. If you give the silent treatment long enough, I guarantee things will not end well. A seemingly small problem can push a whole deal into meltdown mode. That is what comes from not making phone calls and confronting small problems head on along the way.

"Communicate— silence breaks trust."

A lot of employees avoid telephone calls when they might have an upset customer on the other end of the call. Sometimes our receptionist will get one of these calls and no one will want to take the call. Unfortunately, ignoring it will not help what might already be a bad situation. Not answering this call is not acceptable at my company. We want everyone to have a good experience getting a mortgage and not feel frustrated. So if there is no one around, the next voice the caller will hear will be mine. Now, I have an entire business to run. I may not have time to talk to Mr. Jones, but I will talk to him on the phone. If you listen to my conversation, you will hear me say, "Mr. Jones, I completely understand you are very unhappy and you feel everything with your mortgage has gone wrong, but that's absolutely not the case. We are going to get you to the settlement table on time. We just need to have this one item cleared so we can do a good job for you." At that point, it may be the borrower's responsibility to come up with a document or information. We should be glad he called and we were given a chance to address his concerns.

The person at the reception of your office illustrates the culture of the company. This person is a symbol of what you want your company to be. This is a vital part of the company's culture and sets the tone for how visitors feel about your office from their first impression. I must say that we have a wonderful person, Elle, who does an amazing job in representing our company when anyone first enters our office. She is the first face of CLG.

My approach to getting customers' cooperation is different from that of many others because I try to help them understand *why* I need the information and *how* I can help them. I remind customers that I do not make the rules or the guidelines. Fannie Mae or Freddie Mac write the guidelines, which I follow. You have to follow these guidelines and you have to help people understand why you are asking for certain information.

Our CFO, Steven Winokur, is not originally from the mortgage industry, so I had to get him completely up to speed on our industry. I thought Steven's unfamiliarity with the mortgage industry was a huge plus because of everything the mortgage industry had encountered over the last decade. I wanted someone with fresh ideas and a corporate background. Steven came from a huge international company and his accounting terminology can sometimes be too obtuse or technical for me. At times, I must confess, I do not understand what he is saying. So, we came to an agreement. We teach each other. We come from very diverse backgrounds and look at things completely differently, yet we usually come up with the same idea in the end. We have a mutual respect for each other, which is great because we work with each other every day. For instance, when Steven was trying to explain how an accounting waterfall principle works, I had to say, "No, I don't understand that in any way. Why am I not earning what I think I'm earning? Why is the company not making what I think it should be making?" Okay, so we have to pay taxes, and report it in a certain way. Those were the sorts of things that I had to have explained to me over and over.

I still have two operations people who were with me from even before the beginning of Centennial Lending Group. My assistant, Kristi, has been my processor forever and has, over the years, been given tremendous responsibility. She is now my right arm. Over her tenure of more than a decade with me, there have been many laughs and a few tears. Our closing manager, Joy, is close to having been with me for a decade too. About a year and a half ago, Kristi came into my office, crying, because her husband had been transferred and they had to move to Illinois. I was shocked and saddened to think of her leaving. She said telling me she was moving was more upsetting to her than telling her mother. That is the kind of relationship we have had for a decade. It is great to have your employees invested in working with you and to know they have your back. I know that is part of our secret sauce. I have tried to replicate it, but it is hard to replicate. When her husband was transferred back to this area, and they moved home, it was fantastic news. Building a team starts from the top and is a delicate balance; you need to build a solid foundation.

I am a new CEO. My journey to this position has taken many twists and turns. I once was new to the job of post-closer in a new industry of mortgage lending and worked my way, over time, to becoming a seasoned loan officer, and eventually, a top producer. I love to originate loans and see each loan through the process to the borrowers getting the keys to their new home. I think of every loan we do at Centennial Lending Group as being mine. Everyone knows my attitude and I will help in any way. As we continue to grow, I have put in place key managers who know when there is a problem, they have to come talk to me. I am directly involved with the handling of problem loans, as I believe they need upper-level management's input. There are not many CEOs as involved as I am, and I think that is an awesome benefit for Centennial Lending Group.

Part of putting together a great team is having key people in place to handle the inevitable day-to-day situations that creep up on us. I am not a worrier by nature, which has worked very well for me throughout my life. However, as a manager, I have come to realize I tend to worry more when I feel my managers are not worrying enough. As long as my managers and the people who report to them are worried about something, then I know the matter is being looked after, which gives me peace of mind. It was important for me to hire excellent managers for underwriting, closing, processing, compliance, and secondary marketing, who have built-in alarms as part of their personalities. I want my managers to be on constant alert for potential problems. When I do not have to worry about catching everything, I have more time to dedicate to other issues. As a team, I believe we strike a good balance.

A company needs worrier-types in the mix. When we were audited by the Pennsylvania Department of Banking, my then operations manager did not think it was a big deal. In my view, he was taking the audit lightly, which was upsetting and made me nervous. It is the operations manager's job to worry when the company is audited. Because he was not worried, I became superworried. As a consequence, I handled everything. Without that level of concern, however, we would not have been so fine. More recently, we went through a New Jersey Department of Banking audit, and my assistant VP was in charge of that audit. She got deep into the details of it. I knew she was really worried about the audit, which lessened my worry, and we did just fine. Needless to say, a manager who is not worried should not be working at Centennial Lending Group.

I always tell people they can bring me the biggest of problems but they should try to come prepared with a solution at the same time. My CFO once forgot to do a payroll transfer. He neglected to push the button that transfers the funds into the right accounts. That was a disaster, but one that was fixed quickly and easily. If my staff members do not have a solution, we can work one out together. I have no problem with that. However, I need to know my staff tried to come up with a solution first. We can laugh and figure it out, and then, in hindsight, say, "Yeah, that was a really bad one. Let's try not to do that again." This is the key to problem solving: making sure not to repeat mistakes of the past. I think this is what people sometimes miss: laughing a little bit and remembering to be humble. As they try to find solutions to problems, people need to realize we are all human. We will not take risks if we fear making mistakes. I make big mistakes at times, so I definitely live by this dictum.

Mortgage origination is definitely an on-the-job training field. Even people who have completed the classes, gotten licensed, and are full-fledged loan officers can have difficulties. Recently, one of our loan officers came in, dejected. "God, it is hard to generate business," he said. I told him, "It's well worth it. Once it hits, you're going to love it." I know because I have been through it. I have grown from a newbie to a major producer, and I can assure you it is all about confidence.

Having the confidence to walk in, knowing you are great at your job, with a company that backs you, is what it is all about. Then, you can look at someone and say, "If you're not using my company, you're not using the right company." You have to ask, "How can I get you to try me one time so you can see how wonderful my team is at getting a borrower to the settlement table quickly, easily and beyond your expectations?"

Usually, once my loan officers get their first deal, they realize they are good loan officers, and they have a good company behind them. It is amazing to see this relationship flourish. When loan officers come to Centennial Lending Group, we try to give them all the tools they will ever need to do their job to the best of their ability. We cover the expense of business cards, marketing, and their Facebook pages. We do not charge them for any of the social media work we do on their behalf. Heck, we give them a laptop. They know we are behind them and will not desert them. We try to be over-staffed rather than understaffed at all times. I know how many applications come in every day. I know how many loans close each month. However, even if business dips a little, it does not mean I am laying five people off. It means we are just staying the course. I think other companies lay people off as soon as business slows. I refuse to do that, because when business picks up again—and it always does—the company will not be able to handle the workload.

People who work here know if they make a mistake, it is okay. It will certainly be discussed and we will provide additional training so that particular error is not made in the future. If they make a mistake and do not tell me about it, however, that might not be okay. My staff knows. "Tell Sue before Sue finds out on her own." That can only mean trouble. People are human and they make mistakes. I, at times, make huge mistakes. I am even proud of some of my mistakes. The higher the position, the larger the mistake. Nothing is perfect and no one is perfect. You just try to do your best and learn from the mistakes you make. Sometimes a mistake can be the best thing that can happen.

Our goal is to treat everyone fairly and equally. In the past, at other companies, I have experienced unequal treatment. I was loyal and the top soldier. Yet, other people would be brought in for more money, even though their volume was not close to mine. As an employer and manager, I think it is important to show loyalty and fairness, especially when it comes to compensation. While I do not want people to jump ship and move to another mortgage company, sometimes that happens. I am never surprised, though, when the smoke that was blown at them by the other company more often than not does not quite pan out as they thought it would.

Most businesses make many decisions based on how things affect their bottom line. We are no different. I always know our bottom line. I know most, if not all, our numbers, but I tend to focus on revenue and sales volume. Someone once told me revenue heals all wounds, and I believe it does, up to a point. We just need to keep generating it. That is our strategy. We try to have a completely painless process to finish a loan, so we can have more repeat customers and build relationships on solid foundations. If we do that, our revenues will grow. This is my mantra: develop relationships that will continue in the future.

What happens if something is not going correctly in the office or with one of our loan officers? We have a discussion immediately. "What are you having issues with?" I might ask. "Where do you see the need for improvement? What happened at your previous company? What did they do better? What could we do better?" I want to hear the answer to each of those questions. I do not believe there is a company out there that cannot improve on the process it has in place and this includes my company. We have an open mind so we can improve at any time.

Centennial Lending Group is a special place, but there is always room for improvement. At one of our sales meetings, I sat down and said, "I want everyone to finish this sentence with me: Two all-beef patties, special sauce, lettuce, cheese, pickles, onions—" and before I could finish, everyone was saying it with me. Everyone knows this jingle. We all grew up with it. Even if you have never eaten a Big Mac, you still know each ingredient. I said, "What is our special sauce, and what's your special sauce? What do you need in your special sauce to make it taste even better?"

I took a big felt-tip pen and I wrote down every single answer to those questions. The comments were right on target: professional; surrounded with experts in the field; a team; the A-team; a great culture; huge communications; a positive attitude; supportive; creative. They even hit on some of my personal philosophies, including "Pick up the telephone and see what the problem is, even if you don't have an answer." We listed what made us special. The salespeople want to work someplace special and they want to feel special. Listing this makes people aware. They start to see if any one department drops the ball, it causes chaos for, or at the very least puts tremendous pressure on, the next department. If we turn in one rush file, it is no big deal, but when one department is handed five rush files all at once, that becomes hard to manage. The question and discussion become: "How can we avoid spreading the special sauce too thin?" My job is to monitor the special sauce.

Most days I tend to roll with the punches. When I arrive in the morning, sometimes I do not have an agenda, but 9 times out of 10, I know what needs to be done. In the mortgage business, stuff happens, and my staff needs to feel I am in control and will back them. Sometimes I have to back sales, and sometimes I have to back staff. Sometimes, I have to do both at the same time. I may have to sit with my underwriting team and say, "I understand where you're coming from and I understand why you sent out that e-mail, but you do not understand the problems you caused when you sent it." An underwriter may need to make a point but cannot express it appropriately in the e-mail. If another manager were asked to read it over, she might help to make the point more effectively. In those cases, I have to fill in the communications gaps.

Striking a balance is important. I may have to explain to sales staff, "The way this other department voiced its complaint was wrong, but, ultimately, what was said had merit." It is a constant balancing act. You have personalities and some of them are "big" personalities. The difference between sales and operations staff is huge. They have two completely different mindsets. We all need to understand both.

Recently, I had a sticky situation. One loan officer was giving us a lot of rush loans, and I told our sales manager, John, to talk to him. His rush files were creating a bottleneck because they were settling within 20 days. We had to find a better way to manage all these rushes. Not every file should be a mad rush. We had to calm him down a little bit. I knew he was trying to shine, but he would still shine brightly without a ten-day rush on every file. He needed to understand that it is fine to close a file in 30 days. Each salesperson has to understand the effect his actions have on the rest of the company. At any company, you need generals, and you need lieutenants, but you also need foot soldiers. It is essential that everyone at every level feel appreciated. You have to understand where all sides are coming from, and when you do, the results can be amazing for everyone.

Appreciation is a key factor. Both sales and operations staff need to be told they have done a good job, or you can see they are working hard. Over the years, I have learned it costs nothing to tell people how well they are doing. Do you know what saying, "Thank you," costs? Nothing, zero, nada! Do you know how much it is worth? *Everything!* So I keep a box of note cards in my purse, knowing I can write a card to employees to thank them for doing a good job, which shows I appreciate them. I do this all the time. Sometimes, before I go to bed, I send a note to my receptionist, Elle, who is amazing. I thank her for something she did during the day. It is priceless. You can send an e-mail, but sometimes, a quick personal note goes even further.

I can say every employee at Centennial Lending Group is there for a reason. Unless something clicked at the interview, I would not have hired an applicant for a position. We want people to enjoy their time at work. If someone does not "click," something needs to change. Occasionally, we hire people who end up leaving because the position was not the right fit. Those employees may not be part of our culture, or they may not want to work as hard as everyone else does. This is okay, as long as it is recognized quickly.

"Say 'Thank you!' It really makes a huge difference."

I had one loan officer who showed up to a meeting 40 minutes late. She apologized for being late. I was waiting for an excuse, such as her dog ran away and she had to run a mile to find him, or she got in a car wreck, or her tire was low, or she ran out of gas. Instead, she said, "I just couldn't pull myself together to get here on time." This was unacceptable. This was not the culture of respect we value at Centennial Lending Group. Let me tell you, in her place, I would have said virtually anything but that! It showed no ownership.

Appreciation, or even a heart-felt thank-you, can go awry if the rest of your communications are off base. I have learned a great deal regarding how to communicate with others through the Entrepreneur's Organization. This is an organization I joined a few years ago. There are many great takeaways from this organization. Yet the one I feel stands out the most is the way the members give advice without really giving advice. The advice is given, based on personal experience. This is not confrontational. Expressions such as, "You should do this and you shouldn't do that," are avoided. Instead, we say something such as, "Well in my experience, I did it this way," or "What I have found is..." This advice has been invaluable to me. I have changed the way I speak to my staff. I have even changed the way I talk to my children. If, in your critique, you tell a story, it is much easier for the other person to become engaged and remember the story. As you may have noticed, I have a lot of stories. I have covered every facet of my profession, from post-closing to sales and managing, to being an executive. When I offer advice or guidance, I really am speaking from experience. I always try to convey this to whomever I am advising.

One last note on employees: Yes, I want Centennial Lending Group employees to care about their company, but Centennial Lending Group is neither their family nor their home. Our employees do not work much overtime. We are not like some mortgage companies where everyone works until all hours of the night. I want my staff to be home with their families, have dinner with them, and go to their children's basketball games. I want that for Centennial Lending Group employees. I enjoyed having dinner with my family when I was growing up, and it is important for us all to do the same. I cherish my time with my family and try to maximize it. However, if somebody calls me on the weekend or in the evening, I will pick up the phone. I take the call because I enjoy working, but I will have to remember to listen to the voicemail later. It is all about balancing work and home. It is constantly a juggling act, and sometimes, you need to embrace the juggling. I love being with my family and I love my work. When you are in love with what you do, people know it, and it makes life a lot easier.

Corporate culture is vital at Centennial Lending Group. We have developed a specific environment which we try to consistently maintain everyday. Loan officers have a comfortable sitting area and staff members do not work in cubicles. Our offices resemble family rooms, with comfortable chairs and couches, and the walls are painted in colors that make you feel happy and calm. Because we spend so much of our time at the office, I feel this is important. Also, when people come to meet us, whether for a job or a mortgage, they feel comfortable immediately. Some people come in not knowing what to expect. Yet, when they leave, they intend to come back. It is definitely part of our *special sauce*.

CHAPTER 10

Bring Your Toolbox

Years ago, I made a decision to change the way I do business. My business mantra has always been two simple words: *no problem*. At times the issues at hand were minor, but more often they were major.

Big or small, I made sure they would be taken care of without any fuss. "Just leave it to Sue. She'll figure it out."

I made it a point to get out of that habit. It made a huge difference in how I saw myself and how people viewed me and the value I was providing them. I forced myself to drop the phrase *no problem* from my vocabulary. In fact, there *were* problems, plenty of them, and many were very challenging. I substituted, "I don't know how I'm going to handle this, but I'll work on it," or "As soon as I figure out a solution, I'll get back to you." I had noticed before, if you continually say, "No problem," everybody starts to think what you are working on is easy. Sometimes, if people are amazing at what they do, they make it look crazy easy, when this is not really the case. Guess what? The customers move on and do not give another thought to the amount of effort you made to get the results. They walk away thinking there was never a problem in the first place. As a result, they devalue the exemplary service you just provided them. Meanwhile, you probably did not even realize you were the one who created this devaluation mess to begin with by saying, "No problem."

That decision was a big one for me in my career. It helped to propel me to the next level as a loan officer. To this day, I avoid tossing around that phrase. *No problem* should not be in salespeople's vocabulary. Instead, I encourage anyone in sales to say something such as, "Let's see how we can make this work."

I remember how this all came about. One day I was sitting at my desk wondering why certain realtors seemed to think my job was so easy. They insinuated it was a breeze, going so far as to say it was "easy money." Such comments frustrated me to no end. They were simply wrong. Every single file on my desk had some problem associated with it. "What would have to happen," I wondered, "for people to appreciate the value I bring to all of this?" I thought, "How can I accomplish that perception?" I realized I was always saying, "No problem," when, in fact, I should have been saying, "That was an awful lot of work and I really killed myself on this loan." It hit me. I was making my work look easy—too easy, a common issue for people who are great at what they do for a living.

I wanted to do a lot of business, and I wanted to please everybody. That is how my name went from Gap Girl to Go-To Girl. Whenever there was a problem, everybody would say, "Call Sue. She'll make it work." Finally, the pressure on me started to mount. I was not just selling anymore; I was selling and managing people at the same time. I was also entering my 30's and having children. Even when nine months pregnant, I was working long hours and taking on a tremendous amount of stress. It was a wake-up call, a big wake-up call.

I had solidified many business relationships and accomplished a great deal with the no-problem approach. I got a lot of mileage out of it. Eventually I realized whatever success I had achieved as a result of repeating the no-problem line was actually redundant, because the relationship had been established by my actions and competence, not the phrase. It had run its course. In a weird way, it felt as if it were starting to work against me. I already had the backing. I had established my reputation, and now I needed to figure out how to grow my business. How could I get more business? Realtors were already giving me business, so now I had to get business from the borrowers. I had to figure out how to make the borrowers raving fans and sell for me. Raving fans are those who are so happy with the product or service you have provided them, they tell everyone about you and your amazing service.

In 1998, I pivoted more toward personal referrals. From 1994 to 1998, realtors were my only business referrals. The realtors were my customers and my lifeline to all the business I would do in the future. They were my go-to source for building my business. My past customers were an untapped market, I realized, and when I decided to tap into them, the timing was perfect. Rates were going down, and refinancing was rampant. I started to market to my past customers. I told them how hard I had worked for them the first time around, and I now wanted to earn their business all over again. I got in touch with them quarterly, at times even monthly. Today, they still receive marketing materials from me via e-mail, Facebook and Twitter, among other social media, which are very hot and important to us at Centennial Lending Group. We have bought in totally, and find social media to be powerful prospecting tools. Early on, we made a commitment to become frontrunners in the social media arena, which continues to be one of our major initiatives.

We still e-mail and direct mail our past customers, but social media avenues have really helped our business. We use Facebook, Twitter, and Instagram. Everybody knows immediately what is going on. They are great communication tools. When we received our five-star Best in Philadelphia Award, we promoted this accomplishment through social media avenues.

All my friends know I own a mortgage company. If they need help with their mortgage, they know to get in touch with me. Their network is right at their fingertips. When buyers go to the settlement on their new home, we post their picture on Facebook. It is an important milestone in their lives. All the testimonials we receive are posted on Centennial Lending Group's Web page. We also use these venues to educate our borrowers on changes and developments in the mortgage world. Doing so lets us better inform borrowers about the best options available to them when purchasing or financing a home.

When you get a mortgage, you have three options. First, you can go to a bank. Second, you can go to a broker, who actually is a middleman. Brokers are not authorized to order appraisals, nor do they underwrite files. They process the files and then ship them off to a bank. Banks are the businesses that approve the loan, close the loan, and provide the money at the settlement table. They charge the borrower a fee for this service.

A company such as Centennial Lending Group is the third option—and what I believe to be the best option. We are a correspondent lender, which means we take the mortgage application, order the appraisal, and collect money from the borrowers. Centennial Lending Group processes and underwrites the loan. Most importantly, it closes the loan and funds the loan in its own name. The borrower is not charged anything except traditional closing costs for processing the mortgage application. After settlement, we usually sell the mortgage to one of several investors, which is how we get paid. At Centennial Lending Group, we are able to provide all the services of a big bank but with a very personalized feel. I think this is the best option.

Beyond keeping the file in one place, I think this system is superior because the consumer gets the best of all worlds. We are able to shop for the best rate among our various investors (banks). Borrowers get the best service—fast, personalized service. As a correspondent lender, we have total control of the loan at all times. We give world-class service to the borrower and close the loan without ever leaving our office. Turnaround times for brokers and major banks are long right now. A refinance can take months. Centennial Lending Group, on the other hand, can settle loans in just three to four weeks. When everything goes smoothly, we can settle loans in ten days.

When I am selling against the big banks or talking to people about their options, I say, "Go to the big bank and your file will have more frequent flyer miles than you do." I then say, "Or you can come here and get personalized service, and a real person on the telephone. We're going to do it faster and make your life easier. Maybe the rate is 1/8 of a percent higher because we have more overhead at times. Maybe it's because we pay our people more, but we think there's a value to it and we're going to get you and your loan to the settlement table."

The huge banks probably will get your loan to the settlement table—eventually. It is just a matter of how much extra waiting and wondering you are willing to tolerate. How much anguish will you have to contend with? I am not saying we are hassle-free. At times, we will call for lots of documentation, but we always explain why. Consumers today will zero in on the lowest rate and have no relationship with their loan officer. They may not even remember their name. In the long run, that could hurt them. Make no mistake. I would like Centennial Lending Group, eventually, to be big and well branded. It is just that we always want to keep a boutique lender feel in our mindset, never losing sight of how important personalized service is, and will always be, to our customers. No matter how big we become, we want to provide world-class service, every time.

• •

Speed is important in my business. We are always trying to streamline our process. One story I like to share is how 72-hour approvals became not only a reality but also standard policy at my company. It also illustrates how small the world can be. We were making a presentation to a very large realty company, which was in the process of selecting a mortgage company to be its in-house mortgage firm. It was a really big opportunity. We made our presentation and were asked, "How fast can you do a mortgage approval, a loan from start to finish?" I said, "We are really fast. We can settle a loan in seven to ten days." We were told, "That is not the norm," and I replied, "That's correct, that is not the norm. We have in-house underwriting, so we can get an approval and settle between ten days and two weeks. If we need to get a quick mortgage approval within 24 hours, it would be a rush, but we could handle it."

I left the meeting, feeling very confident about our chances of becoming that company's in-house lender, based on our presentation. A company representative contacted us after a few days and said a company in North Carolina had been selected. I was confused. A nonlocal company had been selected and all files would have to be shipped back and forth. It turned out this North Carolina company was chosen because it claimed to be doing something really new in the industry: offering 24-hour approvals on all loans, not just rush loans.

I was skeptical. I knew the name of the company and I belong to a group of correspondent mortgage companies. I picked up the phone, called my liaison there, and asked, "Is this particular mortgage lender a member of our group?" She said yes and gave me the CEO's phone number. It turned out that we had very close family connections in Virginia. Meanwhile, he too had not actually won the business. He would have, but another company swooped in and paid a ridiculous amount of money to get it. The good news, however, was that we had a great talk and eventually, I went down to North Carolina to tour his facility. After that visit, I created a whole new process at Centennial Lending Group, whereby every loan that walks through the door, as soon as we have signed documents, gets a 72-hour approval. The whole mortgage industry had been doing things backward, and this process altered my thinking. We had been asking the processors to predict what the underwriter was going to ask for on a file. A loan application should go to underwriting first and the underwriter should be the one to say what might be needed. This change was neither quick nor easy. In fact, it was a painful process; one that affected each department and is still evolving to this day. Everyone had to buy in, since we were shifting the way we were doing business. I truly felt it was for the best and put the customers (our borrowers and realtors) at ease by issuing a complete mortgage commitment very early in the process. As time goes by, I see more and more mortgage companies leaning in this direction. We always try to put better systems and procedures in place and we devote the necessary time to observing and tweaking them.

A wise man once wrote three words on a piece of paper for me: *good, fast, cheap*. He told me anyone can usually have two of the three factors, but to get all three was not usually possible. I use this guide all of the time. If you want something *cheap* and *good*, it will not be *fast*. If you want something *fast* and *good*, it will not be *cheap*. If you want something *fast* and *cheap*, it will not be *good*. It is a good way to keep grounded when you are speaking to a customer or for yourself. Yet it also helps with leveraging your service.

"Everything should have a system and procedures. We try to make sure the procedures are followed by everyone."

Service is really just one of the factors that help a borrower become a raving fan, which is the ultimate compliment. I love borrowers who become raving fans of ours. I would say 20 percent of our customers fit the raving fan description. The number could very well be higher. It is not unusual for me to receive telephone calls and e-mails each week from past customers. People tend to rave about our services on Centennial Lending Group's Facebook page.

We have amassed a ton of wonderful testimonials that have become our story, our track record, and we love getting them.

CHAPTER 11

Shooting for the Stars

I tend to set high goals, not only for myself but also for everyone at Centennial Lending Group. It is important for everyone to turn those goals into reality. People sometimes ask me how I came up my original goal of doing $40 million of business consistently, as an originator. In the past I would have said, "I just picked the number out of the air." There is a bit more method to the madness than that. I will never lowball our goals; we will always aim high. The reality is I am drawing on years of experience to give me a gut feeling, and those same years of experience have taught me to trust my gut, especially in certain markets. In a meeting last year, when I stated my goals for the company, somebody said we would never hit that number. My reply was, "Let's not take that attitude." I have to feel our goal is well within our reach and we can do it if we all put our minds to it. It might be a stretch, but we will work hard.

Good CEOs must know and understand all the numbers in their business. It is essential to running a business properly. I set these goals by looking at overall market projections. I then factor in how many salespeople we need to hire to hit the mark. Only then will we have to gear up for bringing that volume in. Anyone we hire in the last quarter of the year will be geared up for next year, so the hiring has to come early or it will not help us to achieve our numbers. For example, suppose we set an annual goal of mortgages worth $200 million plus. We take the $200 million and divide it by an average of $285,000 per mortgage, and it comes to about 800 mortgages a year. We still need to drill it down.

Say we have 20 salespeople. I will look ahead and project how many salespeople we may need in the field for the next year. Let us say this number is 40. This could mean doubling our sales force. Then, we have to figure out how we execute that and, in turn, what type of support staff we would need. I would bring all of this to the board and tell them what I had projected over the next year. This can

"Set big goals— business and personal goals! Keep track by measuring them."

be done for any business or sales position. This is what I did on an individual level when I was an originator and now I do the same on a bigger scale, as CEO. Just have a goal and drill it down.

However, my goals have to be realistic. I set goals for the company, I set goals for my children, and I set goals for myself. I tell salespeople all the time to set big goals and write them down. Next, break your goals down further into measurable steps. How many applications would you want to take? How many realtors do you expect to visit, or how many settlements do you need to have monthly? You can do the same thing with personal life goals. How many of your child's football games do you expect to attend? How many family events do you want to have during the course of a year? How many vacations are you planning on taking and where? You need to write it all down. If you do not, you definitely will not hit those goals.

Not all goals are necessarily financial. Years ago, one of my realtors told me my conversational style was abrupt. Often, when she and I finished speaking, she would feel dismissed by me. This was pretty upsetting to hear. That was absolutely not the impression I wanted people to have of me. I did not mean to cut them off. I was just trying to work at a certain pace, which was pretty rapid fire. It was obviously hurting me professionally, though, and maybe, personally as well. I took a sticky note and wrote "S-H-O-R-T" on it and then drew a circle with a line through it. Whenever I spoke to people on the phone, I looked at the note. I kept it posted near my phone for 10 years. If I felt myself trying to shut down the conversation because the information I needed had been shared, I would slow myself down. Instead of trying to say good-bye, I might ask the caller what the rest of her day looked like, or what she was planning to do on the weekend. Nonfinancial goals matter too, especially if they will increase business.

Some of my CEO goals have changed as I have grown into my position. There is an expression— "working *on* your business instead of *in* your business." I am guilty of this crime, of being too hands-on. I thought I needed that as a goal. Maybe I needed to be *less* involved with the daily minutiae. For the past few years, I have been preoccupied with changing the systems and procedures by which we work. As our organization was small, we put systems and procedures in place to help us grow to 50 people. Now we are set up to increase in size to 500 or even 5,000 people with the same systems. Even with substantial growth, our systems and procedures should not have to be changed, just tweaked. We have made sure that if something is not working in any department, I will jump in to try to improve a process. Then, when we bring on those additional 10 loan officers, the process is in place for them.

What I have come to realize is Centennial Lending Group could become as big as some of the bigger banking institutions. It could be as big as any company in the market. When I was a salesperson, I thought about my annual commissions for the year ahead and realized the sky was the limit. Centennial Lending Group is no different. The sky is the limit. We can become a public company, or we can remain a private company. We can have thousands of people working for us. We can be as big or as small as we like. Once you are making money, it does not really make any difference if you do $200 million of business or you do $2 billion worth of business. It really boils down to how the machinery works and the income you make on a per-deal basis. Every company needs to find its profitability "sweet spot". That is the idea behind having a great CFO and a great accounting department: finding out exactly where the "sweet spot" is for the most profitability. Right now, we are just in our infancy. Yet we are working every day on this process because it is so important to understanding our business.

Of course, there is more to our business than systems, procedures, and financial sweet spots. Centennial Lending Group has built a culture around the service side of the business. If we can maintain a culture, then we can continue to move forward. Being approachable is very important to me for the operations and the sales. However, I have noticed if I am having a bad day, the whole staff might have a bad day. The lesson learned is to leave personal issues at home. If I am having a bad day, my bad day has to be finished by the time I walk through the door of the office. It is a very infectious culture, with good and bad. I advise my managers to realize what is going on in their personal lives filters down to everyone else at the company and to try to set a good example.

I give salespeople virtually the same advice in coping with borrowers and realtors in difficult situations. Not long ago one of our originators was having a difficult day with a few loans at the end of the month. He was crazy stressed and was not handling it well, so he decided to go home. I felt this was the wrong solution, so I sent him the e-mail below which truly sums up how salespeople should approach their work:

You are in control of the way you handle every situation. You knew all along this was a new program. No file closing in less than 30 days is going to go flawlessly. This is a classic case of setting poor expectations. I would have said, "I believe we can get to the settlement table, but it is a new program, so we need everyone to be on the same page." You are the only one who can tee it up. The way you handle these issues gives you the opportunity to shine in handling a bad situation. I always prided myself in handling these stressful situations by communicating the glitch and making everyone (realtors and staff) understand I was behind everyone and rolling up my sleeves. Leaving the office sends a negative vibe. In every career, you will have your highs and lows. It is how you handle those situations that sets you apart. You have the ability to do this and the team to back you, but you need to embrace the good and the bad. I am telling you this so you can grow from here. If you look at the glass half-empty, you will always want more and nothing will be right. If you look at the glass half-full, you will see you can

handle this with grace and everyone will understand.
I will even call the realtor with you.

As I look to the future, I envision our growth continuing at a remarkable pace. It is all well and good for a company to become very large, but it is also important to ensure the established service standards are adhered to. Not only is putting the appropriate structure in place paramount but it is also the biggest challenge. Keeping a ship sailing—having it go faster and carrying more cargo—that should be your vision. If you see a crack in the hull, you need to fix it—immediately. Keep the ship afloat. Find the leak early on and fix it fast.

"Make sure you set realistic expectations for everyone involved in the transaction. Practice makes perfect!"

Not long ago we felt the ship's hull was cracking. We had to figure out what was wrong and how we could get to a hundred units in a month without staff members losing their minds. I met with my management team and said, "What made this week so difficult?" They felt the recent personnel changes, specifically in the processing staff, had made it difficult. I said, "That will be discussed at the next management meeting. Right now, we have ten minutes, so I want you to remember how you feel and jot down what you think happened." It is similar to having a baby. Eventually, you forget the pain. Understanding what happened so we can fix the problem and do better next time is very important.

I have a daily report showing me the number of mortgage applications taken by each salesperson. I can see five applications were taken today and who took them. It is a matter of looking continually at a dashboard: how many loans were taken, how many applications went in, how many loans came through underwriting, and how many loans closed. So I always know the flow. I do this because I used to track my business based on applications, and it worked really well. I figured out the main metric I could use on a daily basis to guide me and enable me have a glimpse into the future. I am always looking for data to be used constructively to identify the trends.

The other day, I asked to see all the files of one of our loan officers. I literally went through every single one. Part of being a hands-on CEO is continually trying to improve our system. Maybe I could be cruising along, but I prefer to be digging in and figuring out ways for us to improve. We already provide our customers world-class service, but I am always looking for ways to make it even better. As CEO, I strive to meet the goal of constant improvement. The entire mortgage field works on deadlines. I am trying to get us out of the habit of using the commitment and settlement dates to guide our business. Some companies, when working toward a mid-August deadline, do not even pick up the file until they are well into July. At that point, mid-August still seems eons away. All the other loans take precedence before that one, which is human nature. I am trying to change that culture. Everyone knowing the details of the business and our having constant communication with each other will get us to that point.

• •

I believe most people still want to own a house because they think home ownership makes financial sense. It is the American dream. All of us have gone through rough financial times. I think there will be tremendous benefits for people who have maintained their homes and continued to pay their mortgages in a timely fashion. Good things come to those who do the right things.

I was driving downtown recently when a segment about the American dream came on the radio—only, they talked about it turning into the American nightmare. Could this be? If the mortgage tax credit is taken away, are people still going to buy houses? People will still be transferred. People will have growing families. People will still get divorced, and people will still refinance their houses to take the equity out for any number of reasons. People will always need housing. The housing market will continue to guide our economy for years ahead.

In my opinion, buying houses, getting married and having babies is now more a 30-something activity than the 20-something activity it was years ago. I think the demographic has changed and definitely gotten a bit older since I bought my house when I was 28 years old. People are having children later in life. People are saving up and buying a four-bedroom house with two bathrooms instead of a two-bedroom house. Some people do not like the idea of a starter house. They do not want to buy a fixer-upper. Today, many seem to want the walk-in closet and the three-car garage. Even those who are buying old houses and fixing them up need money to make the upgrades. They tend to be a little older, a little more established. Before taking all of that on, they must have stable jobs, with good incomes. I believe the current economy makes it really hard for one person to handle a house and everything that comes along with it. I see a lot of buyers who depend on dual incomes. Obviously, it is easier to maintain a house and pay for everything when a household has two incomes.

These days, you hear about first-time homebuyers who do not buy a starter home. They buy a higher-level house that, in the past, would have been a second-purchase home, where they would stay for a longer period of time. People are not moving as much. This way, they are not paying closing costs over and over again.

I sell a product 95 percent of Americans need if they want to own a house. Very few people are buying houses with cash these days, although this number does seem to be growing. We occasionally see people with hundreds of thousands of dollars in the bank who are buying a house. "Why," we ask, "have you not bought the house before now?" They were looking for the right house or they sold their house a couple of years earlier and relocated to a different area. Consequently, they did not know if they were going to stay in the area. Now, they realize they are, so they are ready to buy their house. That is a rarity, though, a lucky exception.

The American dream of homeownership might have changed a bit because a house requires upkeep and some people have no patience for it, but it still is necessary. To thrive and continue to prosper, the mortgage industry has to move toward the purchase business in addition to refinances. The demand is there for mortgages. How you acquire the business and how fast you complete it for the consumer are the most relevant considerations.

I always advise people to buy at their comfort level. Mortgage payments tend to get easier no matter what risk the customers thought they were assuming when they purchased a new house—if, that is, their employment status stays the same as it was when they were qualified to purchase the house. Sometimes, to get a reward, you have to take a risk.

Home buying is very future oriented. It is in the compartment in our mind that is looking ahead. We all make plans, and we hope we can make them come true. In some cases, what we accomplish actually exceeds what we had originally projected. In general, we want to come close to what we envisioned. A mortgage helps us attain our dream.

I believe we need to understand the movement of life, the natural ebbs and flows. Eventually, we will have to take things as they come. Obviously, I have plans for the really important aspects of life. I know, basically, what I would like to see happen as my children move along into high school, college, and then adult life. I also have plans for Centennial Lending Group, and as I mentioned earlier, they project 10 and 15 years into the future. However, part of

"The sweet spot is when hard work and opportunity meet."

what makes Centennial Lending Group work is our ability to handle things as they come. Our hair is not on fire day in and day out. If an opportunity comes to pass, then it comes to pass.

We work hard to execute what we laid out. We make progress, and it is very organic, very much in the flow. We really believe when hard work and opportunity meet, anything is possible.

CHAPTER 12

. . . .

Getting Lucky

As I envision the future, I look at what we have built at Centennial Lending Group so far, and what we are striving to achieve going forward. If you have read this far, you know our level of success has been remarkable, but it has not come easily. I could write many chapters about what has gone right and even more about what has gone wrong. When I look back, though, I can honestly say I would not change a thing! Every experience, good and bad, has been a learning experience.

I love the culture we have built at Centennial Lending Group, and I love the brand we have established. I believe our team is second to none, from the people who open a file to those who do the loan processing, the underwriting, the closing, and post-closing, and to the general administrative support departments. I believe our sales people have the tools they need to get as much business as possible. They have what they need to build their future and we have the infrastructure in place to support all the business they can generate. Centennial Lending Group works as a team and our team ROCKS!

I worked hard to put together a team, but we also got very lucky. I believe a major key to success is you have to get lucky. It is all about getting lucky and having the secret sauce. But luck does not just happen. You have to be prepared to get lucky; you have to work diligently to get lucky. You have to keep an open mind to get lucky. You have to be ready, when luck meets opportunity, to put everything together and take advantage of any situation. That is how you build a future. That is what I did at Centennial Lending Group.

At the beginning of the book, I stated success takes a little bit of crazy mixed with a little bit of luck and a lot of hard work. Now you can see why I am the first to say, I am one crazy lucky girl!

• •

For more information on Centennial Lending Group, visit:
http://www.clg-llc.com/

Find us on Facebook!